# KHARIS
## Hellenic Polytheism Explored

~ 2nd edition ~

Sarah Kate Istra Winter

*First edition 2004 printed by Cafepress.com*

**Copyright © 2008 by Sarah K. I. Winter**

All rights reserved. No part of this book may be reproduced by any means or in any form whatsoever without written permission from the author, except for brief quotations embodied in literary articles or reviews.

Printed by CreateSpace in the United States of America

"And then there are the gods. Some guy is running back to report on the outcome of a battle and he's running and running, and he sees Pan in a glade. And Pan says, 'Tell them to build me a temple here.' So he says okay, and runs the rest of the way back. And he reports the battle news, and then says, 'Oh, and by the way, Pan wants you to build him a temple.' It's really matter-of-fact, you know?"

"So there are stories with gods in them. What are you trying to say? That these guys had hallucinations?"....

"I like my theory better," said Shadow.

"What's your theory?"

"That back then people used to run into the gods from time to time."

- *American Gods* by Neil Gaiman

# TABLE OF CONTENTS

Dedication & Acknowledgements................................................5
*Kharis*: Definitions..................................................................7

Introduction.............................................................................9
Notes on Language..................................................................11

CHAPTER ONE. Ancient Greek Religion....................................15
The Myths; Cult Practice; Temples; Religious Roles; Rites of Passage; Miasma; Oaths; Mixing Wine; Music, Dance and Theatre; Oracles; Values; Non-Mainstream and Foreign Cults; Patriarchy and "The Twelve;" Historical "Facts"

CHAPTER TWO. Modern Hellenismos.......................................29
Introduction; Other Pagans, Other Places; What We Take From the Past; Scholarship; Language and Clothing; Religious Names; "Hard" vs "Soft" Polytheism; Citing Sources and UPGs; Community; Priesthood; Ancient Mindset and Innovation

CHAPTER THREE. Kharis through Ritual..................................41
Creating Effective Ritual; Tangible Acts; Hellenic Ritual Types; Festivals and the Calendar; A Personalized Religious Calendar; Animal Sacrifice; Ritual Structure; Offerings; Disposal of Sacrifices; Hymns; Libations; Temporary Festival Shrines; A Festival Day Example; In Conclusion

CHAPTER FOUR. Kharis through Relationships........................63
The Gods; The "Olympians" and Beyond; Ancestors; Heroes; The Nymphs; Other Spirits; Agathos Daimon; Household Religion; Shrines; Holy Places; Prayer; Listening to the Gods; Divination Methods; Omens; Patron Gods; Devotional Acts; Pilgrimage; Everyday Practice; "Everything is Full of Gods"

CHAPTER FIVE. Mysticism, Magic & Mysteries.........................97
Meeting the Gods; Ecstatic States; Prophetic Trance; Ancient Mystics; Acts of Magic; Mystery Cults

Afterword.............................................................................111

APPENDIX I: The Ancient Athenian Calendar and Major Festivals .................................................................... 113

APPENDIX II: Plants, Animals, Places, & Activities Sacred to Specific Gods and Goddesses........................................................... 121

APPENDIX III: Useful Greek Words and Phrases for Religious Practice................................................................................ 127

APPENDIX IV: Results from the Hellenic Pagan Survey................131

Bibliography......................................................................149
Internet Resources............................................................155

About the Author..............................................................157

# DEDICATION & ACKNOWLEDGEMENTS

First and foremost, this book is dedicated to all the theoi and daimones of ancient Hellas, with the hope that it helps increase the breadth and depth of their worship in the future. And of course, to my own cherished gods and spirits in particular, to whom my life is devoted.

I would like to thank my partner, co-religionist, and best friend Sannion, who I first met in the Hellenic polytheist community online. Dionysos brought us together, and I could not be more grateful for his friendship, love, inspiration and support over the years.

I would also like to thank the following people and groups from the polytheist communities who all at different times and in various ways influenced my religious development, inspired me, and/or provided good fellowship: Maureen Reddington-Wilde & Daitales (for my first large-group Hellenic ritual); John Wells & the Cult of Dionysos (for an unforgettable Lenaia, among other things); Apollonius Sophistes; Todd Jackson & Kyklos Apollon; the Meliophis satyrs and maenads; the Pantheacon crew from 2006-07; Aristotimos (whose correspondence has been essential to me these past years); Suz (for some amazing readings); Jolene Dawe & Laure Lynch (both such good friends and so important to my spiritual life); my Livejournal friends; and the members of Thiasos Lusios, Neos Alexandria and Neokoroi. Also I thank my former temple, Kin of the Old Gods, with which I had many of my formative ritual experiences, and my first ecstatic rites.

Finally, I want to thank my mother, Barbara Rachel, for first planting in me the seeds of spiritual exploration and a knowledge of the numinous. I do not think I would be where I am today if it were not for her own religious quest, and for her deeply spiritual soul.

χαρις (transliterated either *kharis* or *charis*)

I. outward grace or favour
II. grace or favour felt, whether on the part of the Doer or the Receiver
V. [in reference to divinities] homage due to them, their worship, majesty

> - definitions from the Liddell & Scott *Intermediate Greek-English Lexicon*

".... the essence of *kharis* is that the god is offered something pleasing. The worshipper establishes with the god a relationship not of strict indebtedness but rather one where the god remembers the gift and feels well disposed in the future." (Pulleyn, 12)

"Men live by the hope of reciprocal favour, *charis*. 'It is good to give fitting gifts to the immortals' – they will show their gratitude." (Burkert, *Greek Religion*, 189)

# INTRODUCTION

"Traditional polytheisms are subject to constant change; that is one of their traditions." (Parker, *Athenian Religion*, 152)

Hellenic polytheism as it exists today is still in the formative stages. This book is a discussion of our ancient roots, our modern religion, and most of all how we can foster a truly deep and personal spiritual practice, in which the gods are a real part of our everyday lives. I am in part a scholar, and therefore will delve into the history of ancient Greek religion, its rituals and beliefs. But I am foremost a devoted worshipper of the gods, and as such I can speak on the practice of this religion from experience.

I think that our everyday spiritual interactions are the heart of Hellenismos. I believe that through awareness of the gods, acts of devotion, and the cultivation of personal relationships with them, we can shape modern polytheism into a powerful religion in our lives, one which is entirely relevant to our environment, but still has strong roots in the ancient customs and mindset.

Throughout this book, I will give my own ideas and opinions on how best to approach the practice of Hellenic paganism. There are myriad viewpoints on how to revive this religion; mine is only one. I will also give a more general overview of the many elements of our religious beliefs and practices, and the issues facing the community. I hope this will be a useful reference as well as a catalyst for further exploration.

This is not an introduction to paganism, or to Greek mythology. This book assumes the reader has a familiarity with the gods of ancient Greece. If you do not, I suggest turning to my bibliography at the end and choosing a few of the entries there to start with. However, I have tried to make this book accessible, without requiring much previous knowledge of the ancient religion or its modern revival. This book is for the person new to Hellenismos, unsure of where to begin. It is also for the person who has been practicing for years, and is interested in making the religion a more integral part of his or her life. Finally, it is for the person outside of the religion, who simply wishes to learn about us, our beliefs and our traditions.

It is an unfortunate fact that most of the information available to us about ancient Greek religion comes from the limited time and place of Classical Athens – and therefore, that was a reasonable place to start our reconstruction, when modern Hellenismos first began. However, there are many other topics to be explored – the religion of the rural areas, everyday devotions, mysticism, household cultus, etc. We are, I believe, in the process of moving beyond basic reconstructionism and finding a balance between that approach and innovation, localization, and personal experience. I hope this book provides some helpful information and discussion on these matters.

I have noticed that modern pagans are particularly devoted to their religion, probably because we have all chosen our paths deliberately and sometimes at a cost, and we do not do so lightly. This is for all of the passionate followers of Hellenic polytheism, always learning and growing, and finding more ways to show the gods our love.

# NOTES ON LANGUAGE

I think the ancient Greek language is an important element of Hellenismos. I will address the various issues surrounding language in our religion later on; here I simply want to provide some assistance for those who may be unfamiliar with the ancient Greek words and phrases I have used throughout this text. I have opted, generally, to use a slightly different transliteration of Greek letters into English than is commonly seen in earlier texts, one which reflects a more accurate pronunciation. There are instances, however, where the correct form would be so unfamiliar as to perhaps cause confusion, in which case I fall back on more common spellings (such as writing Dionysos instead of Dionusos).

Here are some guidelines: Υ/υ is rendered as "u" (instead of the common "y"); Χ/χ is rendered as "kh" (instead of "ch"); Κ/κ is rendered as "k" (instead of "c"); "ae" and "oe" are discarded in favor of "ai" and "oi;" the common "us" endings are replaced by the correct "os." Therefore Oedipus becomes Oidipos, Aeschylus becomes Aiskhulos, etc.

Of particular importance, in my opinion, is the correct spelling and pronunciation (to the best of our ability) of the gods' names. I believe it is a sign of respect to try as best we can to accurately say the names of the gods. These are not just any words which may have changed over time (like most of the pronunciation of the Greek language has); they are proper names. Just think about how you would prefer people to at least make an attempt to pronounce your name correctly.

A common mistake to avoid, if you are strictly reconstructing Greek religion as opposed to some kind of Graeco-Roman blend, is the use of the Roman versions of the gods' names instead of the Greek ones.

Here are a few that are commonly confused, the Roman followed by the Greek: Apollo/Apollon; Hecate/Hekate; Ascelpius/Asklepios; Hercules/Herakles.

Further information on the gods' names and their pronunciation can be found in *Appendix III*.

A few general notes on ancient Greek pronunciation – first and foremost, I must stress that this topic is a matter of ongoing debate in scholarly circles. Different teachers may advocate conflicting methods of pronunciation. There is no absolute and consensual form. Additionally, there were many different dialects in ancient Greece; depending on what region you were in, you might hear the language spoken in a variety of ways. I believe the majority of people these days are working with Attic Greek, but just keep in mind that it was not the only dialect.

The following rules are what I was taught and what I've seen most commonly: Remember that iota [I/ι] is an "ee" sound, and that when viewing a name in the original Greek, there is a difference between omicron [O/o] and omega [Ω/ω] (short and long o, respectively), and epsilon [E/ε] and eta [H/η] ("eh" and "ay", respectively). Unfortunately, in English these differences are often overlooked. Gamma [Γ/γ] is always a hard "g" as in the word "Greek." Also, there is no "h" in ancient Greek – when a word is transliterated as beginning with "h" it means the initial vowel is aspirated, and that is the way it's expressed in English. "Kh" [X/χ] is a common sound (like in *kharis*) and is pronounced similarly to the "ch" in the Scottish word "loch" or the Hebrew word "Channukah" – it comes from the back of the throat.

A guide for vowel dipthongs (two vowels together) is to voice one vowel sound and then the next, but quickly so that they meld into each other – therefore, for instance, alpha-iota (ai) is a short "a" followed by an "ee" sound, creating something like the word "eye".

Unfortunately, there is no general rule for how to accent nouns in Greek, it is somewhat complicated. I have given the accents for some of the gods' names in *Appendix III*. If you are concerned about how to accent other words in Greek, I would suggest buying a copy of Liddell and Scott's *Intermediate Greek-English Lexicon* which may well become a valuable tool in your study and practice.

It is helpful to remember when looking at a word in Greek (or transliterated into English) that there are no silent letters in Greek (unlike English) – if it's there, it's pronounced in some way. For example, while we start our word "psyche" with an "s" sound, in ancient Greek it begins with a "p" sound (the whole thing sounds like "psoo-khay").

Of course, being grammar, there are quite a few exceptions to these rules, but they do serve as guidelines and will result in at least adequate pronunciation. If you wish to know more, a textbook on ancient Greek language may suffice, although it is far better to take a class in person (many universities offer ancient Greek classes). There are also some pronunciation tapes available.

One last word about language – in this book, I use the terms "Hellenic" and "Greek" pretty much interchangeably. While the words "Greek" and "Greece" are far more familiar to most English speakers, they actually come from the word for a single tribe in ancient times, which was eventually adopted as a word for all Greeks. In the Greek language, their country is called Hellas, and therefore we get the adjective Hellenic (you may sometimes see the word Hellenistic used as a general adjective, but that is incorrect, as the word refers specifically to an historical period - dating from Alexander's death in 323 BCE to the death of Cleopatra and the Roman annexation of Egypt in 30 BCE). So for variety, and to be both accurate and familiar, I have chosen to use both of these terms throughout this book.

For more information on the ancient Greek language, see the "Language Reference" section under *Internet Resources* at the end of this book.

# The Greek Alphabet

with approximate equivalents in English

Αα = alpha = a
Ββ = beta = b
Γγ = gamma = g
Δδ = delta = d
Εε = epsilon = e
Ζζ = zeta = z
Ηη = eta = ē
Θθ = theta = th
Ιι = iota = i
Κκ = kappa = k
Λλ = lambda = l
Μμ = mu = m
Νν = nu = n
Ξξ = xi = x
Οο = omicron = o
Ππ = pi = p
Ρρ = rho = r
Σσ (ς at end of word) = sigma = s
Ττ = tau = t
Υυ = upsilon = u
Φφ = phi = ph
Χχ = khi = kh
Ψψ = psi = ps
Ωω = omega = ō

# CHAPTER ONE

# Ancient Greek Religion

# ANCIENT GREEK RELIGION

Hellenismos is the revival of the religion of ancient Greece. While we strive to create a practice that is relevant to our modern lives, we must first study and understand the past. With a thorough knowledge of the ancient beliefs, rituals and overall mindset, we can then modify the religion while maintaining an internal consistency. However, this book is primarily about our current religion, and so an in-depth discussion of ancient Greek polytheism would not be appropriate; there are plenty of books in my bibliography that will give such information. Instead, I will touch upon a few of the elements of the old religion and culture that are important, relevant, or misunderstood.

## The Myths

Many of us learned the Greek myths as children; they are common stories in our culture. In fact, I know many of us first became interested in Hellenic paganism from a love of the myths. The Greek myths are beautiful, complex stories that give us a glimpse into the lives of the gods and heroes. However, it is a common misconception that the Greeks based their religion on these myths. In fact, in practice the myths had rather little bearing on religious beliefs and rituals.

For example, there are plenty of stories of Pan chasing the nymphs, even raping some of them, and generally making their lives unpleasant. From this, one might conclude that Pan and the nymphs are on bad terms and would never be included in worship together. However, exactly the opposite is true: there were many sites in ancient Greece where Pan was honored alongside the nymphs, including the famous Korykian cave above Delphi which belonged to all of them. To the worshippers of these divinities, it seemed more important that they traditionally haunted the same places, and were all spirits of nature, than what they did in the myths. So, when studying Greek religion, it is important to make a distinction between myth and actual practice, especially when deciding how to approach the religion and the gods in our own lives.

It should also be remembered that there are many variants of the myths; one particular story might have half a dozen different versions, some of which diverge significantly from each other. Sometimes we can trace a given myth back to the original, but most of the time it is unclear which version came first, or if instead they all grew up simultaneously in different areas. This can be frustrating at times, but also fascinating. It took quite a bit of studying, for instance, before I found the variation of the famous Theseus and Ariadne myth in which Ariadne is killed at the end by Artemis, on orders from Dionysos. That really broadened my understanding of that story and of Dionysos himself.

Does the fact that myth and religion are not synonymous, and that there are so many mythic variants, mean that the Greeks did not really believe in their myths? That is a difficult question, and one many people have tried to answer. Perhaps, each person believed in the stories that he or she was told growing up, whichever versions those happened to be. Certainly in later times, many educated people declared that the myths were simply allegories. Today, many Hellenic pagans believe that the myths are metaphors, meant to explain some aspect of the gods or natural forces. Others, like myself, think there is more truth in them, and that it is possible that at some time in the past, the gods did indeed make their actions more well known to humans, and even interacted with us more directly. Perhaps some of the stories, for instance, of the gods taking human form were a way of saying that the gods possessed or influenced mortals for brief times in order to interact with other mortals on a physical level. And perhaps other accounts reflect the experiences of dreams or visions. Of course, some could just be entirely the product of human invention.

However, no matter what they believed in ancient times, cult practice (the word "cult" here is used in the older, neutral sense, meaning a group of worshippers, usually of one or several gods) and everyday worship had much more to do with local custom and personal experience than with even the commonly told myths of the gods. Thus it is often said that ancient Greek religion was an orthopraxy, rather than an orthodoxy, meaning that it was more important to *do* certain things than to believe certain things (which is the opposite of the emphasis in monotheistic religions). As the scholar Martin Nilsson said, "The piety of the ancients was expressed chiefly by acts." (*Greek Folk Religion*, 73)

## Cult Practice

Even the rituals, however, varied between cities, as ancient Greece was less a unified country than a collection of self-governed towns that all shared certain cultural and religious similarities. "Demes formed their own religious community and as such celebrated their own festivals and performed their own sacrifices." (Price, 29) This is important to note, as it means that we can keep this diversity in the religion today, and not feel pressured to agree on one "right way" of doing things, or one festival calendar. There was also a marked difference between the religion of the urban areas like Athens, and that of the rural areas populated by farmers and shepherds. In Athens there were large, state-sponsored festivals, plenty of temples, and theatrical competitions that attracted audiences in the thousands. In contrast, the people in rural areas had a simpler religious life, smaller shrines, local festivals, and were focused mostly on the deities that would help them with their livelihoods. This gives us a wide range of options today in how we approach our religion, depending on whether we live in an urban or rural environment, or something in between.

Another important distinction to be aware of is the difference between *polis* religion (that of the city or town one belonged to) and domestic religion, practiced in private in every household. While the festivals and temples were impressive, the heart of the ancient religion could be found in the everyday devotions carried out by ordinary people in their homes and fields. Unfortunately, we do not have nearly as much information on these rituals, but we have enough to extrapolate from, and I will discuss them in depth in a later chapter.

## Temples

An ancient *naos* (temple) was the house of the god or goddess it was dedicated to (and temples were almost always only for one or perhaps two gods, not general religious places). The god resided within, in the form of a cult statue. Therefore, out of respect, the rituals were actually held *in front of* the temple, not within it. A person would only go inside to have a more private, intimate interaction with the god, such as leaving a small votive offering. The temple usually faced east, and in front of its doors there would be a *bomos*, or altar, which was most often a stone block or a pile of stones. Occasionally, the bomos was made entirely of the ashes of previous sacrifices. (For sacrifices to chthonic gods or the dead, a *bothros* was dug – a pit in which to deposit offerings.) The worshippers attending a sacrifice would gather around the bomos, with the leader of the ritual facing east. As a rule, only one big sacrificial festival was held at each temple in a year.

At present, we have no large communal temple buildings at which to hold our rituals. Hopefully, someday that will change (and already some people are being called to set up small public shrines at which they welcome visiting worshippers). But for now, since most of us worship primarily at home, we can treat our shrines or altars there as temples and stand before them to perform our rituals.

## Religious Roles

The head of the household (almost always a male) was responsible for leading the worship and rites of his family. However, any person could participate in a sacrifice, make a votive offering, or visit a temple to pray to the god or goddess therein. No intermediary was needed between a person and a divinity. The concept of priests made familiar to us by the major monotheistic religions did not exist in ancient Greece. Rather, ancient priests "were citizens who, besides their activities in civic life, had the task of seeing to the cult of a god and looking after his temple." (Nilsson, *Greek Piety*, 4) Only rarely did a priest or priestess' life revolve entirely around the god he or she served. A priesthood could be attained by lot, election, heredity, or even by sale, and was sometimes held for a lifetime, but often only for a limited time. A priest or priestess was only linked to one god and usually to one specific temple or shrine – thus there might be a priest of Delian Apollon, but he wouldn't be expected to officiate at rites for Poseidon as well.

In addition to priests (*hiereis* in ancient Greek), there were a number of other religious roles. *Exegetai* were interpreters of religious law. They were self-appointed and not tied to any one shrine, but rather advised any person in need on how to conduct individual or family rituals. Their advice was not binding, and sought voluntarily. *Khresmologoi* were itinerants who kept lists of famous oracles, like those of Bacis or the Sibyls, and would read from them to those seeking answers. They were also self-appointed, and their income was based solely on their reputation. They were not looked upon favorably by many, but were popular enough to make a consistent living. *Manteis* were prophets, those who could foresee the future or interpret the voice of a god. Some were seen as charlatans, but others were respected and renowned, like the Pythia at Delphi.

## Rites of Passage

Unlike the customs we are used to in our culture, priests did not preside over the major transition rituals in ancient Greece, such as birth, marriage and funerals. Those were instead considered family affairs and were performed mostly in and around the house.

The primary ritual associated with a new baby was called the *amphidromia*, in which the baby was officially welcomed into the family by being carried around the central hearth. It occurred usually on the fifth or seventh day after birth. Sometimes gifts were sent by relatives, although generally only those present at the birth would come to the amphidromia. The doorway of the house might be decorated – with an olive wreath for a boy, and wool for a girl.

A marriage consisted of three parts. First, the *engue* or betrothal, a verbal contract between the fathers of the bride and groom. Next, the *ekdosis*, which began what we would call the wedding itself: sacrifices and offerings were made, followed by a nuptial bath for both bride and groom. Then the bride would adorn herself and attend a feast at the family's home. After the feast, the bride would be carried by chariot in a torchlit procession to her new home, accompanied by music and relatives bearing gifts. The bride and groom would then physically consummate the marriage, which was called the *gamos*.

In contrast to the relative simplicity of weddings, funerals were often elaborate affairs lasting for many days and held at considerable expense. On the day after death, the body was washed, anointed, wrapped in a shroud, and crowned with garlands. It was laid out on a bier in the house for a whole day; this was called *prothesis* ("laying out"). On the third day after death, the body was brought in a procession to the cemetery; this was called *ekphora* ("carrying out"). The procession included women who would cry, singe dirges, and exhibit violent displays of grief. At the cemetery, the body was interred, libations made, and offerings left in the grave. Then the family returned home and purified themselves, then sat down to a funeral feast, called a *perideipnon* ("supper beside") because in earlier times it was held at the graveside itself. On the third day after the funeral, food offerings were left at the grave, and again on the ninth day, which was commonly the end of the mourning period.

## Miasma

However, in all of these funeral rites, no priest could be involved because of the *miasma* (pollution, uncleanliness) associated with death. Death was one of the things forbidden in a holy place. In fact, even the gods themselves were said to shun the dying and the dead. "In poetry, Apollo and other Olympians withdraw at the approach of death and do so to avoid its pollution." (Mikalson, 27) Miasma is a complicated subject. It was a very real concern to the ancient Greeks, and there were many laws about how to avoid it, and how to purify oneself if miasma was incurred. Along with death, other things banned in a sanctuary included childbirth and usually sex. At the entrance to sanctuaries, a vessel filled with pure water was placed so worshippers could wash their hands and rid themselves of any incidental miasma before entering. Many Hellenic pagans today do not feel obligated to follow the ancient rules concerning miasma, at least to the extent they were followed in ancient times, though most of us perform at least some kind of small purification before formal ritual (which I will discuss later).

## Oaths

There are, in fact, plenty of aspects of the ancient religion – both minor and significant – that most of us do not tend to practice today. One such activity is the taking of oaths. This was much more common in ancient times, in a variety of circumstances, and it was a religious matter (much like the custom of swearing on the Bible in American courts). When taking an oath, a person would swear by the gods, make libations, and often even sacrifice an animal; it was not a matter taken lightly or done quickly.

## Mixing Wine

Another common practice was the dilution of wine both in ritual and everyday drinking. They would mix one part wine with two parts water in a large *krater*, or mixing bowl, before portioning it out in cups. The Greeks considered drinking unmixed wine to be barbaric. Many theories are offered for why the Greeks diluted their wine, some suggesting that ancient wine was either much stronger in alcohol content or even laced with some other drug; however both of these ideas are highly unlikely. Wine can only attain a certain alcoholic content, well below the dangerous level. And it is just not realistic, in my opinion, to think that every cup of wine was laced with belladonna or some other potentially deadly drug, without any direct mention of this in the extant texts. It is more reasonable to note that the Greeks expected a certain decorum at their rituals and other gatherings, and so wished to slow down the process of inebriation, especially at symposia that would last for many hours, and at which the participants would be drinking steadily.

## Music, Dance and Theatre

Music and dance played an important part in many Greek rituals, although they are not as frequently included in our modern ones (if only for lack of numerous available musicians and dancers). An ancient Greek sacrificial procession would include many musicians such as *aulos* (double pipe) and lyre players. There might also be dances – both simple, rhythmical ones, and more structured pieces to accompany certain songs. There were special types of songs played for certain gods, such as the *dithyramb* for Dionysos, and the *paian* for Apollon. There were also songs and dances for the harvest, and for wine-making. Some of the ecstatic cults were especially known for their groups of frenzied dancers and musicians, such as the followers of Dionysos and Kybele. Although we rarely have such large groups to make music with these days, we can still play songs and perform dances, even if we are celebrating alone, and it would certainly be a way to span the gap between ancient and modern practice. There are some resources for ancient Greek music listed at the end of this book, for those interested.

Legend says that from the usual choruses of boys singing and dancing, there once stepped forward a man name Thespis, who added dialogue to the performance, thereby creating theatre. Theatre as we know it in the Western world comes from ancient Greece, and the Greeks took their theatre very seriously, and included theatrical competitions in many of their festivals. Since there was a god of the theatre, Dionysos, it was naturally a somewhat religious event. Most of the plays we are familiar with today, such as the famous Theban cycle of Sophokles, were once entries in the dramatic contests at the annual Greater Dionysia in Athens, and other large festivals. While we currently cannot afford the spectacle of putting on theatrical competitions, we can certainly attend modern dramatic performances as part of celebrating some of the festivals. It is often possible to find a local troupe performing one of the ancient Greek plays, since they are still very popular.

## Oracles

Another important part of the ancient religion was the institution of oracles. The most famous, and pan-Hellenic, oracle was that of Apollon at Delphi, where the aged priestess called the Pythia would slip into a trance and deliver oracles to those who went through the proper preliminary rituals. Many important decisions by individuals and entire cities were made only after consulting the Pythia. But there were many other oracles across Greece, where different gods would speak to their worshippers through the medium of a priest or priestess, or in some cases a natural event, such as in Dodona where Zeus spoke in the rustling of oak leaves. Today we have no established oracles to turn to, although there are a few members of the Hellenic pagan community that are reviving the practice of prophecy and may eventually become well known and respected enough to create new oracles.

## Values

One of the legacies of the oracle at Delphi is the set of principles called the Delphic Maxims. These were inscribed for all to see at the temple, and were a guide to a proper way of life. They include: know thyself; nothing too much; worship the gods; obey the law; respect your parents; control yourself, help your friends; and many more. There were many other values important to the ancient Greeks, but the key one was *eusebeia*, or piety. Burkert writes: "Plato has Socrates define piety as 'knowledge of sacrificing and praying.'" (*Greek Religion*, 66) Again, the emphasis is on what is done, rather than what is believed. Eusebeia is still valued by modern pagans as one of the most important characteristics a person should cultivate.

## Non-Mainstream and Foreign Cults

In addition to the conventional forms of the religion, there were some non-mainstream cults that diverged from the norm in their beliefs and practices, but were nonetheless part of ancient Greek culture. These began as small groups, but often grew to be entire movements. One such cult was Orphism – the Orphics had their own cosmology, and adopted Dionysos as their foremost god, although their concept of him differed significantly from the standard. The Orphics were also vegetarians, which put them immediately outside the mainstream religion, since they would therefore not participate in animal sacrifice. The Pythagoreans, also vegetarians, adhered to the philosophy of Pythagoras and believed in reincarnation, unlike most Greeks. These examples show that it is entirely authentic for us to have various cults with different beliefs and practices under the umbrella of Hellenismos.

Also authentic to the ancient religion is the practice of including foreign gods within the structure of Hellenic polytheism. There were plenty of cases in ancient Greece where the deity of another culture was brought into Greek religion and made a part of it. Kybele was originally a goddess from Asia Minor who acquired a significant following within Greece. In the Hellenistic period, many of the gods from Egypt found Greek followers, especially the great goddess Isis who became worshipped all over the Roman Empire by many different peoples (Apuleius' *The Golden Ass* includes the Roman's account of being initiated into the Mysteries of Isis). This is not an endorsement of the kind of eclecticism sometimes seen in the neo-pagan community, such as mixing and matching pantheons and traditions to suit one's whims. But there are appropriate ways to include one or two gods from other pantheons in Hellenic polytheist practice without compromising its integrity. The key is to really learn about the system the new god comes from, and how that god can interact with the Hellenic system.

The foreign pantheon most related to the Hellenic religion is that of the Romans. When the Roman Empire conquered the Greeks, they took back with them much of the Greek culture, including the religion. They altered their ideas about their own gods to look more like the Greek pantheon. Therefore, Jupiter became another Zeus, Minerva identical to Athene. Even older pre-Roman gods were molded to the Greek form, in which Faunus became Pan, for instance. Because of this, many people think the Roman and Greek religions are interchangeable. However, there were many differences as well, in the way they practiced, their outlook on the world, and their priorities. Today, Religio Romana (the revival of ancient Roman polytheism) is its own, independent religion, with its own beliefs and rituals. While some people practice both Religio and Hellenismos, most tend to stick with one or the other, recognizing the differences more than the similarities. Nevertheless, one still sometimes sees Greek and Roman gods talked about interchangeably in the wider community; just remember that these gods are understood differently within their respective traditions.

## Patriarchy and "The Twelve"

There are two other common misconceptions that should be addressed here. One is that Greek religion, and by extension the Greek pantheon, was patriarchal. It is true that ancient Greek culture, like almost all cultures of that time period, was inherently patriarchal and that women were not considered equal to men. But the interesting fact is that the one realm where women *could* be respected and play an important role was in religion. Priestesses were as common as priests, just as goddesses were as common as gods (for a thorough examination of priestesses in ancient Greece, I recommend Joan Breton Connelly's *Portrait of a Priestess*). Even in everyday life, women participated in sacrifices, visited temples, left offerings on their hearths. In cult practice and in the myths, the goddesses and female divinities were respected, feared, and loved as much as their male counterparts. The concept that the Greek pantheon was a family "ruled" by the father figure of Zeus is mostly an invention of 19th century mythographers such as Thomas Bulfinch. While the Greek gods were indeed all related and thus comprised a family, it was not so neatly laid out as we are led to believe, especially since there are so many variants of the myths which give different genealogies for some of the gods.

This leads to the next misconception, which is that the religion revolved around "the twelve Olympians." Even in modern Hellenismos, one will often see references to the twelve gods. This is not without some basis in historical practice; for instance there was an altar to The Twelve Gods in the Agora in Athens. But this does not mean that there were only twelve gods, or only twelve major gods, or that every person in ancient Greece would have listed the same twelve Olympians had they been asked. In fact, which gods were the "Olympians" varied by region, and in practice the question didn't appear to be very important to the ancient Greeks. A person worshipped the gods they were drawn to or had need of, whether or not they were part of the twelve. There were plenty of very important and well-loved gods that were never considered Olympians, such as Persephone. In some versions, Dionysos is one of the Olympians (he even brings his dead mother to Olympos and deifies her), but in others he is omitted, and Hestia is counted among the twelve. However, the popular idea that Hestia abdicated her place on Mt. Olympos to make room for Dionysos appears to have been an invention of the writer Robert Graves, as it appears in his work, but in none of the sources he cites, nor in any ancient work I have come across.

## Historical "Facts"

As the example above shows, our information about ancient Greek religion is not perfect. Sometimes the facts get garbled, or misinterpreted by biased parties. Secondary sources written more than fifty years ago (Farnell, Halliday), by those with pet theories to uphold (Harrison, Frazer), or by poets rather than scholars (Graves), should all be double-checked, though not discarded outright (many certainly have solid information and useful insights, but may also be outdated, disproven, or better viewed as metaphor than fact).

Sometimes a new archaeological discovery completely changes our ideas. This can, of course, directly affect those of us trying to reconstruct the ancient religion. Therefore, we must always be flexible and open-minded. We must be willing to change our practices if given a good reason to do so.

A prime example of this is the controversy over the so-called "Snake Goddesses" of Crete. Much is made of these few little statuettes, especially by goddess worshippers. They are often cited as proof of a matriarchal culture in ancient Crete, and certainly have become the basis for some modern religious practice. However, unfortunately, evidence has come to light in recent years that shows that many of these statuettes were fabricated by the 19th century excavators, and those that were real were often changed in some way, or the circumstances and location of their discoveries were lied about (for more information on this specific subject, read *Mysteries of the Snake Goddess* by Kenneth Lapatin).

Now, everyone is entitled to believe anything they choose, but for those of us interested in continuing the religions of the past, it is important to know the facts about those religions, not just our own ideas. And so we might have to change some of what we thought was true. Even some of the things I have written here might someday be disproved, or our ideas about them might change. Everything changes, every religion grows and evolves, and this can be part of that natural process, but we must be prepared for it.

# CHAPTER TWO

# Modern Hellenismos

# MODERN HELLENISMOS

There are many names for our religion today. The most popular are probably Hellenic paganism, Hellenic polytheism, Hellenic Reconstructionism (though this is more limited) and Hellenismos. Every person on this path can choose for themselves what to call it, and what to call themselves. The term Hellenismos has gained popularity in recent years, as it was the Greek word used by the Roman Emperor Julian to describe the polytheistic religion of the late Hellenic world; Julian was advocating a return to that religion after the official institution of Christianity, as we are doing now.

To use Drew Campbell's definition, "Hellenismos is the traditional, polytheistic religion of ancient Greece, reconstructed in and adapted to the modern world." (Campbell, FAQ posted online) The approaches to this process are many, but what most of us have in common is a love for the gods. Since we are all essentially converts, we tend to be more passionate about our religion than people who have religion taught to them or forced upon them. People often find Hellenismos after taking part in other pagan paths (most commonly Wicca) and finding themselves dissatisfied. Sometimes, they come from a direct experience of a particular god or goddess. Others begin with an interest in the Classics and Greek mythology, which leads them to discover that there are people who are actually worshipping the gods of these stories.

As a group, we have some areas of great commonality, and other areas of great diversity. Including every person who might identify as Hellenic pagan in some way, we will find staunch Reconstructionists, eclectic witches, philosophers, mystics, poets, those with a burning devotion to one god/dess, those who are content to perform simple forms of worship every day for all the gods, and everything in between. For more information on our variety of religious beliefs and practices, as well as more mundane demographics, see *Appendix IV: Results from the Hellenic Polytheist Survey*.

## Other Pagans, Other Places

There is still debate within Hellenismos on whether or not to take part in what is termed the larger "pagan community" which would include other Reconstructionist religions, as well as Wicca in all its forms. Some feel that we are so different from neo-pagans (those that do not confine themselves primarily to one tradition, or practice an entirely modern form of paganism) that there is no reason to communicate at all. Others feel that it is important as a minority group to create a unity across all paths. In the end, it is up to the individual to decide how much or little to interact with other pagans. Personally, I feel we would be greatly enriched by opening conversation with paths that are similarly reviving ancient polytheistic traditions, such as Asatru and Kemeticism (Norse and Egyptian paganisms, respectively), because we might be able to learn a lot from each other.

Another topic that is frequently discussed these days is the revival of paganism within Greece itself. There are, by their own count, thousands of Greeks who are fighting to legalize the worship of the ancient gods in the country in which it first began. The Greek government has been denying them the right to build temples and pursue other expressions of their religion, due to the heavy influence of the Greek Orthodox Church. Of course, those of us in the rest of the world support their efforts. The only conflict arises from a few of these groups (*not* by any means all of them) who believe that Hellenismos is a religion that should only be practiced by those with Greek blood. It is an unfortunately divisive position to take in such a small religion still in its infancy. They might do well to remember that as far back as the 4th century BCE, the Athenian orator Isocrates said, "The name Greek is no longer a mark of a race, but of an outlook, and is accorded to those who share our culture rather than our blood."

Most of us, with or without Greek ancestry, believe that anyone can love the gods and worship them, regardless of race, ethnicity, gender, sexuality, or any other characteristic.

## What We Take From the Past

Some of our beliefs today actually contradict those held in ancient Greece. We may be reconstructing the Greek religion, but we are not reviving the entire culture. Certain ancient assumptions are now rejected for being prejudicial, and this is widely accepted as being a wise balance to the process of Reconstructionism. Therefore, for instance, we do not advocate the ancient practice of slavery, and we believe that women are equal to men. Practicing an ancient religion does not make us ancient Greeks.

Along those lines, there are many gray areas within Reconstructionism, where there is disagreement as to how much to borrow from the ancient practices. As Drew Campbell writes, Reconstructionism "is a methodology for developing and practicing ancient religions in the modern world. Reconstructionists believe that the religious expressions of the ancients were valid and have remained so across time and space. We believe that it is both possible and desirable to practice ancient religions—albeit in modified form—in the modern world." (Campbell, FAQ posted online) That caveat, "modified form," is where much of the confusion and debate lies. How closely must we follow the ancient ways? How much can we change or add to the tradition while still keeping it authentic?

These are difficult questions; I propose that the best way to go about it is to thoroughly immerse oneself in the lore of ancient Greek religion, and then begin to extrapolate from there, once a solid foundation has been established. At times, one must simply go with one's gut as to what makes sense in the religious practice. However, because this should not be a religion for scholars only, and because not everyone has the desire or time to educate themselves on the minutiae of ancient practices, some of us are beginning to condense this knowledge into something useful to others. This book is my attempt, after years of study and practice, to discuss my own ideas for how to craft a meaningful religious life that is both consistent with ancient Greek paganism and has room for change and growth.

### Scholarship

A note, first, for those who are interested in reading the academic works on ancient Greek religion. It is crucial to develop a sense of what constitutes solid research, as opposed to one scholar's biases or personal opinions. Unfortunately, to do this you really have to read a wide array of writing on the subject, and eventually you pick up on which ideas are common and which are unique, what is based on fact versus opinion. To help in this task, it is useful to be a member of an online forum or study group where you can ask others their opinions about certain authors or books.

Also, keep in mind that anything written prior to the last few decades may have flaws and should be weighed against more recent scholarship before being taken at face value. Not only has some of the archaeological evidence discovered since then changed what we know, but older authors tend to have some pretty strong biases. Often you'll find paganism discussed as if it were a primitive notion that was thankfully set straight with the advent of monotheism. Or the author will try to connect disparate practices into one unified theory, like the members of the "Cambridge School" including James Frazer and Jane Ellen Harrison. On the other hand, some of the more recent works have their own problems, like an overemphasis on feminist theory to the detriment of objectivity. Of course, everyone has their biases, and they can still produce quality work, but you just have to take everything with a bit of salt, at least until you can confirm it with other sources.

## Language and Clothing

One of the current issues in Reconstructionism is whether or not one should learn the ancient Greek language, and use it in ritual and prayer instead of one's mother tongue. There are, I think, good arguments on either side. Speaking the ancient language creates a link to our spiritual ancestry. It is the language in which our gods were first spoken to. Perhaps the gods themselves even prefer it (as they often prefer other things of Greek origin, like certain foods or types of music). On the other hand, the ancient Greeks were merely speaking their natural language, not some special ritual tongue. And it is difficult to pray extemporaneously in a language other than one's first, especially one as complicated as ancient Greek.

My own solution thus far has been to use some ancient Greek words or phrases, especially in formal prayers I use often, but to use English in most of my interactions with the gods.

One exception is for the ancient hymns, such as the Orphic or Homeric Hymns – hymns are traditionally considered offerings in themselves, not merely fancy prayers. In my opinion, it seems a more elegant and beautiful offering to use the original language (if possible) rather than a mediocre translation of such. There is a sound, a rhythm, that just can't be matched otherwise. Going to the effort to at least learn the pronunciation and practice reading it (or even better, memorizing it and fully understanding it) is an extra level to the offering. But again, this is regarding hymns, not personal prayer.

I also feel it is important to try to pronounce the gods' names properly. It seems logical to me that any being would like to have their name said correctly, and again, these are the names, the sounds, by which they were called for millennia.

Aside from religious practice, it would be a good idea to learn some ancient Greek because Greek terms are used frequently in academic works (and even by modern polytheists), especially when there is just no real equivalent in English. Also, as any linguist will confirm, learning a language gives you a unique insight into that culture's mindset, something all of us would benefit from as we revive an ancient religion. One who wanted to go further into the study of the language might even one day be able to read primary source material in the original Greek!

Another decision that must be made is whether or not to dress in ancient clothing styles when performing ritual. I think this used to be more common than it is today. My survey (*Appendix IV*) indicated only a small percentage of people are frequently dressing in clothing like a *khiton* or *peplos* for their prayers and rituals. While it is another thing that reminds us of our spiritual heritage, it is not considered necessary by most. The ancient Greeks certainly didn't dress in costume for their festivals, they simply dressed in their nicest clothing, which we can do today with modern clothes. Especially in our daily devotionals, it makes no sense to change into something unusual just to make a libation. However, if one wants to wear Greek style clothing for some rituals, there doesn't seem to be much harm in that, either.

One nice compromise is to wear a crown of leaves and/or flowers (called a *stephanos*) with one's regular (or formal) clothes for festivals or big rituals. The ancient Greeks loved to wear these crowns, and it's a way to have that connection to the past and still be rooted in the present (especially if you make your stephanos from locally picked foliage and flowers).

## Religious Names

Many Hellenic pagans these days have taken special, religious names and use them instead of their given names when doing ritual, communicating to other pagans, etc. Occasionally, they are just screen names in the online world, or nicknames, but often the bearers feel a deep connection to their new names. Some have questioned this practice, wondering if perhaps we are simply mimicking other modern pagan paths such as Wicca, where the majority of practitioners take new names upon joining. However, I think there is a better reason behind it. In many religions, converts will take a new name to symbolize their new faith (sometimes even changing it legally). Since we are all essentially converts (almost none of us have been raised in a Hellenic pagan household) it makes sense that we might feel drawn to take a new name as a badge of our new path. Especially as we live in a society where our religion is not the norm, therefore our names can mark us as members of a different group.

I am not advocating that we all take new names just to do so; it's a very personal choice. But I think it is a valid one too. A religious name can show one's connection to Greece, to a patron god/dess, or something similar. The name I use in the Hellenic pagan community, Oinokhoe (changed slightly from my original spelling, "Oenochoe," to better reflect the Greek), means "wine-pourer" and thus refers to my relationship with my patron god Dionysos. I also have a more private name that I only use in personal ritual. I find these names remind me of my role, my god, and my religion whenever I use them. However, plenty of people seem perfectly satisfied using their given names and feel no need for special ones, which is fine too.

## "Hard" vs "Soft" Polytheism

Judging by my survey, a large percentage (though less than a few years ago) of Hellenic pagans believe that the gods are real, distinct, individual beings with their own histories and personalities. This viewpoint is called "hard polytheism."

In contrast, some prefer a sort of "soft polytheism" which could include beliefs that the gods are interchangeable with those of other cultures (syncretism), or that they are all facets of one (monism) or more greater beings (an example of this is the common Wiccan tenet that all gods are the God, all goddesses are the Goddess), or even that they are archetypes or symbols.

To be clear about my own beliefs and biases, I am a hard polytheist, and therefore all my practices and philosophies emanate from that core belief. I respect anyone's right to believe differently, but I cannot say I agree.

Which viewpoint is closer to the ancient Greeks' is often debated. From my reading, I would say that it seems that most ancient people truly believed in the gods as distinct beings, but as the culture developed some people, most notably the philosophers, began to form other ideas about divinity. It also seems clear that at least some people had no trouble equating the gods of other pantheons with their own, believing them to be the same god if they shared some characteristics. For instance, an ancient Greek person who learned of the Norse god Thor might infer that it was just another name for their own god Zeus, both being in control of lightning. A strict hard polytheist would disagree, and say that all of these gods, from all the pantheons, are separate beings. Each person must decide on their own what they believe.

### Citing Sources and UPGs

There are times, however, when it becomes necessary to distinguish between what was done or believed in the past, and what is a modern (especially a personal) innovation. For the sake of clarity and honesty, Hellenic Reconstructionists are encouraged to cite sources if they are claiming something to be of ancient origin. This is often interpreted by those outside of the Recon movement as snobbery, or at least too much bookishness. But there is a good reason for this rule of thumb. We are trying to make something living, but we are using the ancient religion as a foundation. In order to adequately judge the ancient mindset, and extrapolate from there, we must know what is old and what is new. It does not mean that only ancient things are valid, simply that there is a difference. (And the difference is due not necessarily to the antiquity of the origin, but to the longevity of the practice or belief, the number of people who subscribed to it, etc.)

This is especially true when it comes to changes or additions that are the result of one person's ideas, rather than a general consensus of the community. The former are called UPGs, which stands for Unusual (or Unverified) Personal Gnosis (whereas some call the latter PCPG, which means Peer-Corroborated Personal Gnosis). The term seems to have originated in the Asatru community, but has been adopted by many pagan paths to describe anything from random thoughts to revelations concerning the gods or ways of worship.

For instance, if you have a dream or vision in which you see a god associated with an animal with which he was never associated in myth or ancient practice, you have had a UPG. You might very well feel moved to include this new concept in your worship of the god. You might also want to tell others of your revelation; however it is considered proper form to identify your belief as a UPG, thus distinguishing it from ancient lore. Then people can make up their own minds as to how valid they think your UPG was; they may even take it up and it may become part of the modern tradition, or it may stay your own private idea.

I believe UPG is an essential element of any reconstructed religion; it keeps us from being merely a re-enactment, but rather a living tradition whose followers interact with their gods and thus will inevitably learn new things about them. However, I do still prefer to distinguish between ancient tradition and modern, and to be able to knowledgeably judge the validity of any new idea.

## Community

The ways in which our modern tradition is developing are interesting. Because we are all so spread out geographically, the only point of connection with other Hellenic polytheists for most people is the internet. We have created a community, or one might say many communities, completely virtually. Therefore, ideas can be discussed, practices adopted, all while the participants remain solitary in "real life." It is good that we have any community at all, but many lament the lack of physical meeting with other Hellenic pagans. Community, and group rituals, were a large part of ancient religion. Even at the most basic level, most people had their families to practice with. These days, many of us lack even that.

I think that a good place to start building community now is on a small level, by creating religious groups focused around one god or specific path (even if they are only online for the moment), or which gather worshippers from one area to meet face to face. We can still have a sense of larger, general community on the big discussion lists and forums online, but the more meaningful interactions, I think, come in smaller groups.

A group of Hellenic polytheists that do ritual together regularly is called a *demos* in the organization Hellenion (after the word for a district in ancient Greece) and an *eranos* in the group Neokoroi (which has connotations of a shared meal, a kindness or favor, and a club). A group that is devoted to one particular god is often called a *thiasos*, a word that originally was mostly restricted to Dionysian groups but has since been expanded.

There are quite a few demoi/eranoi and thiasoi currently in operation at least online, and some which physically meet. There have also been some larger "real-life" gatherings of Hellenic polytheists over the past few years, and more interest has been accumulating in meeting each other, all of which I think is a good sign for our future.

## Priesthood

One issue facing these groups, and the community in general, is the issue of priesthood. Some feel that we need priests for a variety of reasons: to lead ritual, to oversee legal events like marriage, to present a good face to the rest of the world which expects a religion to have priests. Some feel that priests are only appropriate in the ancient sense – to be keepers of the temples, and to lead large sacrifices at festivals, neither of which are applicable to our religion yet. Some people believe that priesthood is a personal vocation, something between a worshipper and their god/dess. Some see it as a communal role.

In any case, if we do wish to have priests, the problem becomes how to certify them, and by what criteria we could judge a person. So far the whole issue is sort of taking care of itself – some people simply self-identify as priests of their gods, some are not interested in the role, and some wish to go through a training program to become priests, such as the one offered by Hellenion (which is just one organization within Hellenismos, not representative of the whole religion). There are also plenty of other ways one can serve one's gods and community: through becoming an exegete (such as those in the group Neokoroi), being a mantis or diviner of some sort, keeping a public shrine, writing books or devotional poetry, running a group, etc.

## Ancient Mindset and Innovation

Whatever choice is made on these issues, it is important to understand the ancient mindset before proceeding, if we are to claim any relation at all to the beautiful religion of ancient Greece. It goes beyond just the facts of what was done in each circumstance. It's not just about ritual form or myth variants. For instance, in ancient Greece a libation was always poured out for the gods, even if it was also shared by the worshippers – it appears that the underlying belief was that the liquid must actually be surrendered to be an offering. However, in the Norse tradition, they toast to the gods instead of libating, and drink all the liquid themselves – they believe the gods can still benefit from the act. That may seem like a small difference, but it's those small things that make the various cultural traditions different, that make Hellenismos what it is. This extends past ritual and even to theology: the Greeks, for instance, saw the spirits of ponds, streams, trees, etc., as all female (the nymphs), whereas some other cultures believed they could be male or female.

Once we are familiar with the ancient mindset, I believe it is appropriate to innovate. After all, we have an incomplete record of ancient religion, and much of what we do know is difficult or impossible to do today. I just think such innovation must be done carefully, and always with the ancient tradition in mind. Otherwise, we might as well be creating a religion from scratch, and while that may be a valid type of spiritual path in itself, it is not what we're looking for if we've come to Hellenismos.

For those who balk at the idea of diverging from the ancient tradition, I propose that it is entirely within the context of that tradition to innovate. "The Athenian state turned to the oracles of Zeus at Dodona and of Apollo at Delphi especially on religious questions, for approval of the founding of a new cult, *for introducing or changing sacrifices*, or for change of statues in sacred lands or other sacred property." (Mikalson, 88; emphasis mine) While we may not currently have state oracles to ask, we can still do divinations, and ask the gods for guidance in our efforts to revive this religion. At least we know that even in ancient times, additions and changes were made, as they must be to any religion that is not stagnant.

# CHAPTER THREE

# Kharis through Ritual

# KHARIS THROUGH RITUAL

Ritual is the primary way that humans interact with the gods, across cultures. It is the language of our communication with them. Ancient Greek ritual can almost always be classified as an expression of *kharis*, or reciprocity. "The bond between man and the sacred is consummated in the continuous exchange of gift for gift." (Burkert, *Greek Religion*, 35) Therefore our formal rituals are primarily about beseeching and thanking. Some might mistake this process as a crude form of essentially paying for good fortune; but it is more subtle, and more long-term, than that. "Like other systems of gifts and counter-gifts, the Greek ritual system assumed choice on both sides. Gifts to the gods were not a way of buying the gods, but of creating goodwill from which humans might hope to benefit in the future." (Price, 39) Just like you might sometimes buy your spouse flowers for no reason, and that act creates a more loving and charitable bond between you both, so do we give to the gods, knowing they will also give to us when it is right.

## Creating Effective Ritual

Before I discuss the various aspects of Hellenic ritual specifically, I want to address some points about ritual in a general sense. Just knowing the external details of our rituals isn't enough, in my opinion – we must first consider what makes good ritual, both for us and for the gods.

First one must identify the purpose of ritual. Ritual is how we communicate, not only with the divine, but in our other interactions as well – "by ritualizing we make contact with animals, foreigners and gods." (Driver, 15) Only, with the gods we must first figure out how to dwell in the same space together, before communication can occur. Therefore in a spiritual context, ritual provides the means to do these things, as well as the substance of the communication itself (e.g., asking, giving, praising, etc.).

So good ritual needs to bring a person closer to the gods. Which means that it must take into account certain psychological and even physiological factors involved in being human. Even those of us who are deeply spiritual people cannot usually simply flip a switch in our minds and be in the right mental and emotional state to perceive the gods. A ritual therefore must be structured in a way that helps us move from our normal state of mind to what is generally called an altered state of consciousness. This doesn't necessarily mean we must attain a full trance state or anything of the sort - but ideally our awareness of the spiritual world should be enhanced. Effective ritual "not only presents the invisible but also offers conditions that make the perception possible." (Shorter, 108)

A certain type of atmosphere is therefore required for a ritual to reach full power. This is in some ways superficial – it may for instance include darkness, candles, music, incense, special clothes, etc. – but the point is that it signifies to the people involved that this is not ordinary experience, this is something special, removed from the mundane worries, joys, and cares of the everyday. Now, of course it is possible to put too much emphasis on this atmosphere and create a 'ritual-ish' feel without any real substance. So along with everything I say, one must not forget that the gods are at the heart of this, and these things are done only to facilitate a meeting with them.

"[Mircea Eliade] called sacramental rituals....'doors to the sacred.' Every sacramental ritual, he said, is an invitation to a religious or sacred experience. An invitation, which you may accept or not." (Mike Nichols, online discussion at ecauldron.com) I believe it is not only we who must accept or decline this invitation, but the gods as well. Our hope, of course, is that the gods will attend our rituals, accept our thanks, grant our prayers for assistance, and in general just grace us with their presence. Here are a few things that, in my opinion and experience, make a ritual more effective towards that end.

*Holy silence.* "Koimeson stoma" is the Greek call for silence at the beginning of the sacrificial rite. There's a good reason for this even today, especially in large groups. Having people chit-chatting before and even during a ritual is distracting and often ruins the devotional atmosphere and intent. There should be a short period of time between setup and actual start of the ritual for everyone to stop talking and get ready both mentally and spiritually for what's about to happen.

*Preparation.* In addition to the period of silence, there should be other preparations made stretching back as much as 24 hours before the ritual, depending on how important it is. For instance, fasting for even half a day beforehand will cleanse the body and clear the mind. Bathing (and dressing in clean clothes) just before the ritual is appropriate both for purification and to indicate the formality of the event. At least an hour before you even begin the setup for the ritual, turn off the television, stereo or computer and turn your mind to religious things. Perhaps read some of the hymns to yourself, or think about your last experience with the god in question. One should also endeavor to keep one's mind lightly on the subject of the ritual all day long, from the time one wakes up. These things will mentally and physically prepare you to truly focus within the ritual itself.

*Sensory triggers.* Using the same lighting, music, incense, etc. each time you do ritual creates patterns that your subconscious will begin to recognize quickly, making the entrance into the proper state of mind easier with each recurrence.

*Repetition of acts/words.* The word ritual usually implies repetition; a ritual done often should use the same set of acts/words, at least to an extent, to build up associations. So that eventually, all you have to do is X and you're in the right ritual mindset instantly. Rituals should make internal sense, and follow a basic form each time. "Like language, rituals have a certain grammar, a certain syntax that it needs [sic] to follow, a certain order." (Nichols) Repetition within the ritual itself is good too (such as a simple chant, call-and-answer, etc.).

*Spontaneity.* Repetition does not preclude spontaneity. There should be room for both tradition and for personal experience of the divine, which is naturally going to change somewhat each time. One should be able to add to or even change the ritual if it seems appropriate at the time, within reason (i.e., without compromising the goal or meaning of the ritual).

*Emotional poignancy.* "In many rituals strong emotions are engendered and consciousness altered. Not infrequently there is a feeling of 'loss of self'....and a feeling of union with the other members of the congregation and even more embracing entities." (Driver, 152) We are human beings and we relate to things emotionally as well as intellectually, spiritually, etc. Ritual has the power to bring joy, sorrow, fear, hope, and to entirely transform a person's heart. Add elements that have emotional resonance with you personally, or with your group, and encourage an emotional response to the gods' presence.

*Familiarity.* While respect should always be maintained, a certain level of informality may be appropriate when doing ritual for gods you are on close terms with. For instance, having a meal to which the god is invited, and conversing with him/her in a casual manner (even if it concerns very serious topics) can enhance one's feeling of intimacy with the god.

*Comprehension of participants.* Everyone should know what's going to happen, and why, beforehand. Explanations should not be part of the ritual itself; the meanings of words and actions can be discussed before and even after, but not during. Again, this detracts from the focus and makes it more of a performance than a ritual. Which leads me to...

*No spectators.* Everyone should be involved - even if it's just throwing a handful of barley, or repeating a prayer, everyone should have some way of participating.

*No scripts* (with the possible exception of reading long passages or hymns that would be very difficult to memorize). Again, this is not a play, it is a sacred act. How can you be fully in the moment of contact with the divine if you're looking down at the paper in your hand every two seconds? If this means that the ritual is simplified more so that everyone can remember what they need to do and say, so be it. Personally, I think many things can be spoken extemporaneously anyway, and there is rarely need for fancy words.

*Simplicity.* There are certainly appropriate times for the pageantry of complex ritual, but for most things simple works best – less room for mistakes, more mental space to actually pay attention to the gods instead of the ritual itself. Brings into focus the real purpose of the ritual.

I truly believe that paying attention to these points will greatly increase the likelihood that the participants of any ritual will reach that state of "ritual consciousness" necessary for a real experience of the divine. Which will then make their offerings, prayers and all other communication that much more powerful and meaningful.

## Tangible Acts

An important aspect of ancient Greek ritual is that it involved tangible expressions of the worshippers' purpose. Good intentions, thoughts, and feelings were not considered to be enough on their own. Sometimes pagans these days feel that since the gods know what is in our hearts, we do not need to show it outwardly, but that is a thoroughly modern idea, and one that is in my opinion influenced by the philosophy of Christianity. The ancient pagan mindset was geared toward actual actions and gifts. One of the dangers of the modern attitude is that it is then too easy to not do anything much in the way of worship. After all, if the gods just want you to have the right feelings, then you don't have to do anything, it doesn't matter if you're too busy to do a festival or don't want to spend your money on an offering instead of something for yourself.

I'm not saying that people who believe this do so in order to escape responsibility, but I do think that it can lead to a more laissez-faire attitude than the gods deserve from us. As Todd Jackson said on the HellenicPagan internet discussion group, "The tangibility of Hellenic worship is one of the things I find most appealing about our faith. To my thinking, it simply makes it real, rather than merely sentimental. After all, the Gods' gifts to us aren't just sentiment. Why should they accept mere sentiment in return?"

Do the gods actually require sacrifice, or benefit in some way from what we give them? There are some pagans who will say with surety that the gods no longer require sacrifice, that it is outdated, and that it is preposterous to think that they need anything from us. However, that seems to me a result of modern sensibilities rather than an understanding of the gods and our interaction with them. A quick study of polytheistic cultures around the world will show that most, if not all, believe that their gods require certain tangible things from them. I do not believe that somehow all these cultures are wrong, and only now do we realize what the gods really want, or don't want. At the very least, who doesn't like to receive an external expression of someone's love and gratitude? On your best friend's birthday, do you just think of them fondly, or do you throw them a party, cook their favorite foods, give them gifts? I believe that the gods have given us fairly clear instructions on the types of things they find pleasing (for whatever reason), and it would be negligent of us to ignore that.

## Hellenic Ritual Types

So, having said all that, how does one go about performing Greek ritual? Well, there are many ways, ranging from the smallest libation to the largest festival. Because the ancient Greeks were so fond of festivals and big sacrifices, I will begin with these; however they are not the only way to properly worship the gods, and there are plenty of options for the solitary Hellenic pagan, which I will discuss later on. Also keep in mind that most of the festivals can be pared down to the essential parts and simplified for solitary practice. A theatrical contest can become watching a play, carrying a statue in procession to the river can become washing it at home in front of your altar.

You might also wonder what circumstances warrant ritual for the gods, in other words, when and why do we do this? Theophrastus gives three reasons sacrifices should be made: "in order to honour the gods, or to thank them, or to ask them for something good." (Versnel, 46) So not only is it appropriate to ritualize when we need something or when we are grateful for a gift given, but also simply to show the gods our love, devotion and respect.

Some of us who are not staunch Reconstructionists wonder how important it is to keep to the ancient ways, to do rituals the way they were done two thousand years ago. While I think there is plenty of room for change and innovation, I also believe that keeping at least some of the ancient traditions is important, and it is what makes us Hellenic pagans as opposed to anything else. After all, in ancient Greece "it was above all the observance of rituals rather than fidelity to a dogma or belief that ensured the permanence of tradition and communal cohesiveness." (Zaidman, 27) To revive those same acts, those same rites, is to take up the torch of the ancient tradition, from those who first worshipped our gods.

## Festivals and the Calendar

Large, state-sponsored festivals were a prominent part of ancient Greek religion, especially in the cities. Each region had its own festival calendar, its own list of favored gods, its own traditions. Today, most of what we know of the ancient festivals comes from Athens. We have a fairly complete ritual calendar from ancient Athens, and only some hints of the festivals of other regions. Therefore some people wish to follow the Athenian calendar entirely, since it exists, and others think it less authentic to do so since in ancient times each area would have had its own. On the other hand, it's difficult to start from scratch, and create entirely new festivals while keeping none of the old.

I propose a middle ground, where we learn from the Athenian calendar and retain some of the basic ideas, but also begin to create new festivals that are more relevant to our own religious lives. For instance, if you have Hermes as a patron you will notice that he is almost entirely absent from the Athenian calendar; so you may wish to create a festival in his honor. Or you might find that the alignment of the ancient calendar would require you to celebrate a harvest festival at the wrong time for your climate, in which case you might want to shift the date.

The ancient calendar was based on a lunar system – the month began at the first sighting of the new lunar crescent, and the days were counted from then until the dark moon. Some Hellenic pagans find it difficult to follow this lunar system when our modern calendar is solar-based. They might wish, for instance, to switch Apollon's holy day from the 7th of each lunar month to the 7th of our solar month. However, I will point out one advantage of the lunar system – it has a real astronomical meaning. In other words, the 7th of the lunar month is always the same thing: the 7th day of the waxing moon. Whereas the solar month is more arbitrary. Seeing as modern calendars that show the phases of the moon are fairly easy to obtain, I think holding on to this custom of the lunar days (at least in some circumstances) is a good way to keep some of the ancient tradition that is meaningful.

One way to add additional festivals that have modern relevance is to modify existing civic holidays to a religious purpose. For instance, in America we have Memorial Day, on which we honor those who have died in battle. That is remarkably similar to the ancient Genesia festival, and certainly a concept the ancients would have understood. So if you wanted to feel more aligned with the rest of your culture without neglecting your religious duties and beliefs, you could honor the dead in a Hellenic manner, but do so on the civic Memorial Day.

Creating new festivals entirely from scratch is a difficult process, especially if you want to keep within the ancient mindset. The best way, I believe, to do this is to thoroughly study the festivals we do know of, understand the underlying concepts, recognize the key elements, and then incorporate all of those things into our new festivals. For those interested in this process, and for those who simply wish to carry out the ancient Athenian festival calendar, I have provided a list of the *heortai* (seasonal festivals) and when they occurred, along with some basic information about how the calendar worked, in *Appendix I*.

Notice that many of the Athenian festivals fall into some basic categories, which might help guide you in creating your own festival calendar: there were festivals of the agricultural cycle, of the human life cycle, for purification, and for specific gods (or one aspect of a god, or even specific cult images or statues in specific temples). It was also common for a festival to arise in commemoration of a past event – for instance, a polis that had been saved from a plague after making prayers to Apollon might create a festival in his honor. This is one of the best reasons for creating new festivals, that roots them to our modern time and place – if you have had some powerful experience with a god/dess in the past, you might mark the anniversary of the event with a festival that revolves around it.

Keep in mind, as well, that such a full and busy festival calendar does not have to overwhelm you. In ancient times, the average person would not necessarily have attended every single festival in the area. You can choose to only celebrate those festivals that have the most meaning to you. However, I will add that I think it is important to make some commitments and not leave it all up to your mood on a given day. Meaning that once you decide to celebrate a certain festival on a certain date, you should keep that commitment to the gods.

Along with the basic ritual structure which I will discuss shortly, most festivals had additional activities which we can still perform today (at least given a large enough group). For instance, some festivals culminated in theatrical contests, where various plays were presented. Obviously most of us do not have access to a number of playwrights, actors, and a theatre – but at the very least we could go view a few plays or even movies. Sometimes there would be a musical competition instead, or an athletic one (the original Olympic games were a festival at which the athletic contests eventually gained greater prominence than everything else). The ancient Greeks were very fond of *agon*: a contest in competition for a prize. With some creativity this concept can still be expressed at our festivals today.

## A Personalized Religious Calendar

After years of experimenting and researching and ritualizing, I decided to set down a festival calendar for myself. Of course, I had been celebrating festivals before then, but it was a somewhat haphazard process. I tried to follow the ancient Athenian calendar, but felt uninterested in many of the festivals, or some were timed completely wrong for the climate where I live. There were gods I wanted to do ritual for that had no extant festivals. And on top of all of that, I have a very personal spiritual life which includes a few non-Hellenic gods and spirits, and I wanted to include them as well. So once I was at a point where I felt that I knew enough about the ancient tradition to take it a step further and make a festival calendar relevant to my own life, I began that process (one which is still in the stages of refinement today, after several years). I am discussing it here to give an example of how one might go about this, rather than to suggest that anyone else adopt any particular ideas.

First, I set down a pattern of monthly observances. In ancient Greece, certain days of the month were always set aside for certain gods. Following this tradition (including the use of the lunar calendar, which I prefer), I created some of my own holy days for the gods I worship most. So I kept the 4th for Hermes and the 7th for Apollon, and then I added the 9th for Dionysos (in this case because I found a reference to a Dionysian group in ancient times meeting on the ninth of each month). I decided upon the 27th for the nymphs, loosely based on a sacrifice from Erchia. I kept the 2nd for my agathos daimon, and added the 5th for another daimon I am close to (because it was on the fifth of a month that I first encountered him). I tried to make each innovation have at least some meaning behind it so it wasn't completely random.

I cannot possibly describe all the festivals in my personalized calendar here, because there are over thirty of them. It is not necessary to have so many, but I love ritual, and this seemed like a reasonable amount to me. Enough to keep me in active worship, without being overwhelming. Enough to honor all the gods I hold most dear, in their many aspects, to note the changing of seasons, to commemorate important events in my spiritual life, etc. Anyway, I will choose several to discuss here that should give an idea of what the overall calendar is like.

Since I am foremost a Dionysian, many of my festivals are for Dionysos. Some are ancient, some are from the collection of new festivals created by the Thiasos Dionysos a few years ago, and some are entirely my own invention, or a combination thereof. So for instance, instead of the ancient Oskhophoria, I celebrate the grape harvest when it is accurate for my local area, as part of a new autumn festival called Skenia which also commemorates Dionysos' travels in India. And I celebrate the modern Meilikhia (feast of gentleness) but at a warmer time of year to correspond with the atmosphere of the festival.

I had to create all the festivals for Hermes from scratch, since he is only mentioned once in the Athenian calendar, within the Dionysian festival of the Anthesteria. I created three days for

Hermes scattered throughout the autumn and winter (on the fourth of various months), celebrating my favorite aspects of his: Enodios (on the road), Eriounios (luck bringer) and Psukhopompos (guide of the dead). I also created a couple of festivals for Apollon (even though he has Athenian ones) which focus on his oracular role, since that is how I relate to him most prominently.

Some of the new festivals are entirely personal. Others are actually ancient festivals with no known date. I have also incorporated a few festivals with pagan roots but entirely modern expressions – Mardi Gras could be a Dionysian revel (of course) and Halloween is a day of the dead not unlike the day of Khutroi during the Anthesteria.

Finding activities to do during all of these festivals isn't very hard. In some cases, we even know what was done in ancient times. But when that's not an option, it just takes a little creativity to match the ritual to the spirit of the festival. For the Meilikhia, for instance, I do things that express the soothing aspect of Dionysos' nature – listen to beautiful music, share grapes and figs with the god, drink wine slowly throughout the day, have a long bath, etc. For the Hermaia Eriounia, I celebrate Hermes' luck-bringing traits by doing a little gambling and praying for good luck in general. On the festivals for the nymphs (I've created four, each focusing on one type) I go to wild areas and build shrines for them. This is all, of course, in addition to the traditional prayers, sacrifices, etc.

I have seen more and more individuals and groups creating similar personalized and/or localized festival calendars recently – which is, after all, the way it really was in ancient Greece – and I think this may become the norm in years to come.

## Animal Sacrifice

The most common and widespread form of ancient Greek ritual was animal sacrifice, called *thusia* (a word which is usually just translated as "sacrifice" and often misunderstood). Today, this is a very controversial topic. Some feel it is outdated, or at the least that it will reflect badly on us as a group. However, I maintain that it is an entirely valid form of worship, as long as it is done appropriately. As loaded as the term "animal sacrifice" is these days, we may forget what it really entails. It is in reality not much different than the laws of kosher slaughter in Judaism (a rabbi must bless the facility, and ensure that the animal is killed in a certain manner, and then the animal is consumed as food). Likewise, a Hellenic sacrifice is performed in a religious context, the animal is killed quickly, and the meat is consumed by the participants. In fact, in ancient times, attending a sacrifice and receiving a portion of the meat was the only way some poorer citizens were able to eat meat at all; in essence it was a form of social welfare, since the animals were provided by the richer citizens or the state.

Now, most of us today do not even have this option, as we do not live on farms or know how to humanely sacrifice an animal. But should the opportunity arise, I do not believe it is antiquated or unjust to perform this ritual. For those of us who want to continue this tradition but do not have access to farm animals, a common substitution is to buy meat at the supermarket, and then at the appropriate time in the ritual, cook it and offer a portion to the gods, eating the rest yourself.

If you are a vegetarian, that is a perfectly valid path within Hellenismos as well, since as I mentioned before some major cults like the Orphics were vegetarians. In that case, you could perform most of the ritual and substitute an offering of first fruits or something similar instead of an animal. Feasting with the gods is important, no matter what is served.

Traditionally, when an animal was sacrificed, only the bones wrapped in fat were offered to the gods, and the meat was eaten by the worshippers. The explanation for this practice lies in an ancient myth: the Titan Prometheus (who often sided with humans instead of the gods) attended a communal feast between men and gods. He convinced the men to divide the animal into two piles – one with bones and fat, and the other with the savory meat. The inedible pile was then presented in a way that made it more attractive, and Zeus was thereby tricked into choosing that as the gods' portion. Outraged, Zeus declared that men and gods would no longer come together for such feasts, and from then on humans sacrificed animals on their own and offered a portion to the distant gods – the same portion that Zeus chose.

The gods reportedly appreciate the fragrant smell of the burning flesh, and do not need the meat itself since they do not live on food. Occasionally, mostly in rituals for chthonic deities, the entire animal was burned in the fire – this is called a holocaust sacrifice. It may have been done this way because the chthonic gods were thought to have different needs than the others, or because it was more of a sacrifice in our modern sense of the word, meaning that something of value is given, since an animal was certainly very valuable in ancient times. The animals that were most frequently sacrificed, in either manner, were cattle, sheep, and goats - very rarely pigs, as in the cult of Demeter and Persephone, and also rarely birds or fowl.

Ritual Structure

The preparation for any festival or ritual is simple but also important. First, one should wash in pure water; I think for a formal ritual it is best to fully bathe or shower beforehand, but at least washing your hands is necessary (more on this practice below). Second, one should dress in clean clothes; whether these are dressy modern clothes or ancient Greek clothing styles is up to the individual. And third, one may don a crown of flowers or leaves. This last thing is not strictly necessary, but is a simple and understated way to remember our history without feeling too much like we are in costume or putting on a show.

The basic form of a traditional thusia, or sacrifice, is thus: The participants move in a *pompe* (procession) to the temple, then circle around the bomos. Everyone washes their hands in the *khernips*, which is pure water. The priest or officiant speaks a prayer (more on prayer in the next chapter) out loud to the gods or specifically to the god involved in the ritual. Everyone throws a handful of barley on the altar as a first offering. Incense is also placed in the fire on the bomos, thereby sending sweet smelling smoke up to the gods (like the scent of the roasting meat, this is what they enjoy).

The animal is brought to the priest, and a bit of hair is clipped from it and also fed to the fire. Then the animal is slaughtered by a professional - the *splankhna*, or inner organs, are roasted, a few pieces are burned for the gods, and the rest of the meat is cooked and eaten by the worshippers. Sometimes cakes, broth and wine are also offered. The priest receives the skin of the animal as payment. It is believed that a burst of flame on the altar during the sacrifice is a sign of divine presence, which is of course a goal of the ritual. As Plutarch said in the *Moralia*, "It's not the abundance of wine or the roasting of meat that makes the joy of sharing a table in a temple, but the good hope and belief that the god is present in his kindness and graciously accepts what is offered."

A note on khernips (pure water): purification was very important to the ancient Greeks. The gods were not to be approached with any stain of miasma. This meant, at the very least, washing the hands in clean, pure water beforehand. It could be obtained naturally, from a spring, the ocean, or rainwater, or it could be made pure. The latter can be accomplished a few different ways –

by plunging a burning branch into the water, by adding sea salt (which appears to be a modern tradition, intending to make it akin to ocean water), or some sources say by adding rosemary. Perhaps a good combination of these methods would be to put a burning branch of rosemary into the water, accompanied by a pinch of sea salt. A simpler but acceptable solution would be to use bottled spring water (as long as it's not processed with chlorine or other chemicals like some brands are).

Obviously, if the worshippers' hands are put directly in this water, it will eventually become unclean. A solution, if you want to keep a large amount of pure water on hand indefinitely, is to only pour some of it out onto the hands, thereby keeping the reserve pure.

One final note – you may see in modern Hellenismos the use of the phrase "hekas, hekas, este bebeloi" (let all profane ones depart) at the start of rituals. From what I can tell, there is no precedence for using this as a 'banishing' phrase in general Hellenic ritual. It appears to have its origins within the Eleusinian Mysteries, where it was used as a directive for anyone harboring miasma to leave (rather than applying to spirits or anything of the like). It was popularized by Drew Campbell in his 2000 book, and since then can be heard at many Hellenic rituals. Personally, I do not feel it is really appropriate for a Hellenic ritual, as it seems to be trying to fill the place of a circle-casting or warding from neo-pagan ritual, which has nothing to do with the Greek religious mindset (speaking here only of sacrificial-type rituals, rather than magical ones). In any case, one should be aware of its original context before deciding whether to accept the modern usage.

## Offerings

There are plenty of other types of offerings besides meat, all of which are important and meaningful, either on their own or in addition to animal sacrifice. One major category of offering is 'first fruits,' which is traditionally a selection of the first harvested plants, but can also include other food, flowers, wreaths, money, locks of hair, and models of perishable items (which can therefore be placed in a sanctuary indefinitely). Incense is a common offering in ancient and modern times. As Burkert says, "to strew a granule of frankincense in the flames is the most widespread....act of offering. (*Greek Religion*, 62)

Another large category of offering is votive, which means offerings in fulfillment of a vow, but often is used to describe any devotional gift. These can include statuettes of the gods and of animals, tripods, vases, rings, clothes, armor, masks, oil flasks, cups, reliefs and almost anything else you can think of. "Neither is there anything in the world which cannot become a votive offering." (Rouse, 352) A special type of offering is to give the god an unusual object. An example of such might be a beautiful stone or shell you find on the beach, that seems naturally fit to be a gift to a god. Or something which is not often found, like a snakeskin, or is entirely unique, like a piece of wood that seems to be in the shape of an animal.

Some offerings are specific to certain gods or even particular festivals. The *thargelos*, for instance, is a stew made of harvested vegetables and offered to Apollon at the Thargelia festival. Similar mixtures are actually rather common offerings, and are called *panspermia* in general, meaning all-grains. A similar concoction is offered to Hermes at the end of the Anthesteria. And even today in the Greek Orthodox Church one can sometimes find panspermia called kollyva being made to honor the dead and the ancestors. Another specialized offering is the *eiresione* – a branch of olive or sometimes laurel, hung with wool fillets, ribbons, and other objects. Originally the eiresione was the mark of a supplicant, but it became part of the Puanepsia festival and was carried in procession by children. (For more about these festivals, see *Appendix I*.)

It is not necessary to spend a lot of money in order to offer something special and worthy to the gods. While expensive gifts are nice if you are able to afford them, the cost is not as important as the sincerity, dedication, and consistency of your offerings. A story is told that there was a man who had made many costly and lavish offerings to Apollon, but was told by the Pythia that the truest worshipper of the gods was instead a man in Arcadia who garlanded his household statues each month and made modest offerings at all the festivals.

## Disposal of Sacrifices

A problem facing modern Hellenic pagans is how to dispose of sacrifices. In ancient times, perishable items were usually either burned or buried. Today, we could either bury our sacrifices in the backyard if possible, or burn them on the stove, in a small fireproof dish on the altar, or even outside on a barbecue grill. If no other choice exists, they can be thrown away, but I recommend wrapping them in something to keep them from entirely mingling with the rest of the garbage. Obviously, the last thing you want to have is an offering rotting on the altar, so it is important to dispose of it in a timely manner, however you do it.

Permanent offerings were often left in the sanctuary. Periodically, the more humble of these (such as clay figures and crude votive objects) were collected and buried nearby, and broken objects made of metals like gold were melted down and reshaped in a manner still used for the god. Now, if we choose, we can leave some of our non-perishable offerings as permanent gifts to the gods by keeping them on our altars or shrines, or even by leaving them somewhere special such as at the base of a tree or in the ocean (assuming this wouldn't be polluting to the natural area).

## Hymns

Many people are not aware that hymns were considered to be offerings in themselves in ancient times. Both the writing and reciting of a hymn are gifts to the god involved. For those not inclined or able to write their own hymns, plenty of ancient hymns exist in translation, and are perfectly suitable to use both as offerings and as prayers. The most popular are the Homeric Hymns and the Orphic Hymns, but there are plenty of others, such as the works of Callimachus or Pindar's Odes.

It is likely that in ancient times these hymns (as well as epic poetry and other types of composition) were actually chanted or sung, possibly in the way a Jewish cantor recites the Torah. However, I think that speaking, chanting or singing the hymns would all be acceptable. If you can find them (and read them) in ancient Greek, that would be a special offering (as I mentioned in my discussion of language in ritual), but again it is entirely appropriate to address the gods in our native language as well.

## Libations

The last common type of offering I will discuss here is the libation. It is one of the simplest and easiest offerings to make. There are two basic types of libation: the *sponde* and the *khoe*. The sponde, from what we understand, is first poured out in part for the god, and then sipped by the worshipper. In this way it is shared, much the same way as the sacrificial meat is shared between god and worshipper.

The khoe on the other hand is poured out entirely, similar to a holocaust offering, and likewise is usually made in honor of the dead or other khthonioi.

When making a large number of libations successively, it is considered traditional for the first (and sometimes last) one to be given to Hestia, to honor her place of importance as the hearth (whether that be the hearth of one's home, of the community, or even of the realm of the gods). Though there is only limited evidence for this practice in ancient times, and it may have been a custom in only a few areas, it is commonly practiced today.

Common liquids used as libations include wine, water, milk, olive oil (although this is not, I believe, drunk by the person) and honey, but others such as juice, beer, hard liquor, and even soda would not, I think, be inappropriate, depending on who was the recipient of the drink. Libations are generally poured directly on the ground (or in the case of river or ocean deities, into the water), although modern worshippers often find it more practical to pour libations into a cup or other receptacle on the altar, and then later dispose of the accumulated liquid outside. I've also heard of people who keep a small container of soil in which to pour libations (wishing to feel a more immediate connection to the original practice), and then occasionally replace it with fresh soil and leave the old outside somewhere.

## Temporary Festival Shrines

Sometimes it is difficult to practice our religion as a solitary, without a community, without temples, etc. Festivals can sometimes feel lacking in activities when one is alone, even though there are many things to do (which I'll address shortly). Years ago, I found myself looking for something I could do alone that would symbolize each individual festival and satisfy my sense of ritual and my obligations to the gods. What I came upon is the practice of building small, temporary shrines for each festival. I did not invent this, but rather I noticed other Hellenic pagans doing it, and I have been doing it occasionally for festivals for years, without really pausing to consider why; it just felt right.

Analyzing the practice in context, it still makes sense to me. Ancient Greeks would go to a god's temple to celebrate that god's festival, but we do not currently have temples available, and our regular home shrines may not work well as the focus of a festival for a specific god or event. So why not create a small bit of sacred space which honors that god and gives them a place to inhabit for the duration of the festival, in much the same way as they were believed to inhabit their temples in ancient times. This shrine can become the home base for the ritual, the place to set up offerings and pour libations.

Creating the shrine is also a devotional act in itself. Carefully choosing which objects will be part of it causes you to really think about the god in question and all of his or her attributes, as well as the reason for the festival. For instance, on the Oskhophoria – which celebrates the vine harvest and Dionysos – the shrine could include grapes, a bottle of wine, a statue or mask of Dionysos if you have one, silk ivy or grape leaf garlands (which are readily available at every craft store), a glass or bowl in which to pour libations to Dionysos, as well as the items needed for basic Hellenic ritual (purified water, barley, etc.). It can be as simple or ornate as you wish. You don't even have to have a space specially set aside for such a shrine - a small folding tray table can be covered with a cloth and erected anywhere for that one day, or even only for a couple of hours while you celebrate the festival.

You may wish to leave the temporary shrine in place for at least a few days, to remind you of the festival and the god(s) involved. But you should respectfully dismantle it before the next festival (at the very latest), and in the meantime clear away any perishable items such as food offerings so that the shrine remains clean and fresh (as you would with any other shrine).

## A Festival Day Example

If you are still having trouble visualizing what a festival day might consist of, here is an example. Since most of us are currently solitary, I will talk about only one worshipper, but it would be even better with many.

Let's look at the Thargelia festival, which commemorates the birthdays of Apollon and Artemis. This festival was originally two days long, but we could collapse it into one day to suit our purposes. The Thargelia tends to fall in May – if you were going by the ancient lunar calendar, you would figure out exactly what days correspond to the 6th and 7th (or just the 7th, for a one day festival) of the month Thargelion, but if you are working with a modern calendar only, you might choose May 7th, since that still has some meaning.

Before starting the day, you might choose to bathe specially in order to purify yourself, and put on nice, clean clothes. You could also adorn your head with a wreath – of laurel if possible, but any flowers or leaves would suffice. You could build a small shrine for the festival, as described above, including images of Artemis and Apollon, places to set the offerings, libation drinks, etc. The shrine can also function as the place to keep the objects that belong especially to this festival.

The first element of the ritual is the expulsion of the pharmakoi. Since we do not have the ability (nor necessarily the desire) to choose two people to literally drive out of the city, we can instead make dolls or drawings of a man and a woman, declare them the scapegoats, and treat them symbolically as the ancient pharmakoi were treated. They can rest on the altar, be offered food and drink, and then when the time comes, either be thrown out of the house or destroyed in some way, with a prayer made to send all pollution with them. I tend to personalize this ritual, especially since I'm not doing it as part of a large community – I attach to the pharmakoi symbols or words indicating things I would like to be purified from myself, and pray that these things are consumed in the fire that burns up the pharmakoi.

After your home is cleansed by this act, you can proceed to the basic sacrificial ritual. The procession to the shrine, washing your hands with khernips, saying a prayer to Artemis and Apollon, throwing barley on the altar, burning some incense. Assuming you cannot actually make an animal sacrifice but wish to do something symbolic, you might cook a piece of meat and offer it to the gods. This is the time to feast in the company of the gods, so having enough food prepared (and wine, if you can) for a proper meal is a good idea. You might also supplement or substitute the animal sacrifice with the vegetarian thargelos, or you could choose to leave that for later.

The thargelos is really a simple dish and can be made from any number of different ingredients; it's best if they represent the types of grains, legumes, and vegetables that grow in your area at that time, but any combination of those types of foods will do. I just make a simple stew or porridge, adding laurel leaves in honor of Apollon, some olive oil and perhaps some honey. Then I leave a bowl of this stew on the shrine (later disposing of it properly, as discussed above). You could make extra and eat it as the ritual feast, but make sure that Apollon's share remains untouched.

Now we arrive at the agon aspect of the festival. Traditionally on this day, there were hymn-singing contests. If you do not have enough people for a competition, you could at least recite or sing a hymn to Apollon and/or Artemis yourself, and let the gods judge its merit. I think a nice selection can be found in the Orphic Hymns – if you can find the original (which is given in the Athanassakis translation) and know enough of the language, you could even recite them in Greek.

That is the end of the celebration. If you wanted to draw it out longer, you might find some other appropriate activities, such as attending a choral concert, or you could at least spend the rest of the night in quiet contemplation, enjoying the presence of the gods.

## In Conclusion

Here we have the most basic elements of Hellenic pagan ritual. You may be wondering why I have not included, like so many other pagan authors do, ritual scripts in my text. The reason is that I do not think they are necessary, and I want to de-emphasize the idea of dramatic-type scripts within our ritual structure. Ritual in Hellenismos is simple and can be done without a lot of special words and props and roles. A procession to the altar, the washing of hands, a toss of barley, a hymn read, an offering made. These acts speak for themselves, we do not need fancy speeches to accompany them.

If you want to write words to go with a rite, that is perfectly acceptable, but not necessary. If you want to delegate certain things to various participants, that is also fine (in fact, there were plenty of roles in a big ancient sacrificial ritual, down to basket-carrier), but these rituals work just as well for the solitary worshipper. I think the focus should be on a religious practice that can be done anywhere, with minimal preparation or special items. In fact, meaningful worship can be practiced even without an altar, without a hymn ready, etc.

In the next chapter I will speak on the importance of personal relationships with deities, how to go about fostering these, and how to build a meaningful spiritual life every day within the context of Hellenismos.

# CHAPTER FOUR

# Kharis through Relationships

# KHARIS THROUGH RELATIONSHIPS

"Greek belief incorporated everything that was due to the gods: sacrifices, prayers, hymns, dances, purifications, that is to say, all the 'rites' – the recognized practices, which were in conformity with what it was seemly to say and to do.....But 'belief in the gods' also meant that one lived with them, had dealings with them, sought out their company. Socializing with the gods, cultivating them, in both senses of the expression – both devoting a cult to them and maintaining amicable relations with them – frequenting their altars, getting along with the divine powers: all were commonsensical ways of saying that one believed in the gods, that one dealt with them socially...." (Detienne and Sissa, 168)

"Hellenism, like other religions, is and always has been the response of human beings to what they perceive as the actions of the divine in their lives and in the world. It is easy to forget that all we know and can ever know about the gods comes through the immediate and subjective experiences of people like you and me. These experiences are not well served by expository prose, which is why people use the language of ritual, of art, of poetry and song and dance to express their wonder and gratitude. Our first-fruit offerings, our libations, are our own way of saying what Hellenes have always said to the gods: 'Please' and 'Thank you.'" (Campbell, 24)

I believe that the heart of this religion is not the ritual forms or the historical reconstruction (although those are important) but rather the gods themselves. Being a hard polytheist, I believe in the existence of the gods of all religions, but I have chosen these gods, the Greek gods, because they have touched me personally. Who can really explain why we gravitate towards one pantheon, or one specific god, over another? It is not a logical process most of the time – it is more akin to falling in love. If you have chosen these gods, or if they have chosen you, a priority should be learning more about them – not just from books, but through personal experience. Developing a relationship with the gods is putting kharis into action on a personal level. This relationship (or relationships) can be as close or distant as you want or feel comfortable with, but however it is expressed it is crucial to the practice of Hellenic paganism.

## The Gods

So now it is necessary to discuss the gods and other divine beings of Greek religion. Remember that this is not a mythology book, and I am not going to go down a list of gods and their attributes and stories. There are plenty of fine books on that subject, my favorite probably being Kerenyi's *Gods of the Greeks*. But I do think there are some important points to touch on here.

We often slip into the mistake of thinking of the gods by their most well-known functions: so-and-so is the goddess of ___. This is wrong on two levels. First, the gods are much more complex and nuanced than a simple title will imply; each god and goddess has many functions, many attributes, many stories that show their myriad facets. Secondly, it is important to understand that the "Greek gods are persons, not abstractions, ideas, or concepts....We may say that the experience of a storm is Zeus, or that the experience of sexuality is Aphrodite, but what the Greek says is that Zeus thunders and that Aphrodite bestows her gifts." (Burkert, *Greek Religion*, 182) This is, I believe, a crucial aspect of the ancient mindset. The gods are in everything, not just as a metaphor, but in reality. Beginning to see that in the world around you is a good first step towards greater closeness with the gods; but more on that later.

It is often asked if the Greek gods are omnipotent, omnipresent and omniscient, the way the monotheistic god is supposed to be. My answer to all of these is no – in fact, I think that one of the things that sets polytheism apart from other religions is that our gods are not these things. As for omnipotence, I should point out that if the gods are all real individual beings, they are likely to have conflicting opinions and wishes at times; this is confirmed by the myths. If they were all omnipotent, how could they all get their way at once? How could they take different sides in a war, or all vie for the same thing (like Paris and the golden apple)? As for omnipresence, there is a difference between being everywhere all at once (omnipresent) and being able to *go* anywhere immediately, or possibly even appear at more than one place simultaneously. The latter is how I believe it works for the gods. In fact, I submit that the ancient Greeks themselves didn't believe the gods were everywhere all the time, since most prayers and hymns started with a call to the god to come from wherever they were at present to be there with the worshipper. As for omniscience, I think it is clear that the Greek gods were never thought to know everything. Even Apollon at Delphi was said to be conveying (through the prophetess) the wisdom of his father Zeus, and Zeus in turn was still bound by the weaving of the Fates.

So how can we know anything of these gods? Well, honestly we can never be certain, and it would be hubris to think we understood the nature of the gods entirely. But we can at least learn something from the wisdom of countless generations of Greeks who worshipped these gods, and the gnoses of our own times. We might not really grasp how they relate to our world, how they function within it and yet sometimes seem outside of it. We might debate on how much, if any, the gods truly interact with us, or even care about us. But at least we are trying to understand, making the effort to know these incredible beings we call gods. As C. Derick Varn said on the HellenicPagan internet discussion group, "If anything, Hellenismos seems about reciprocity and as the Gods witness our lives, they allow us to witness theirs, even if it goes beyond our understanding or even the limitations of our view of the physical world."

## The "Olympians" and Beyond

The divine world of the ancient Greeks was not limited to the twelve gods we hear about most often today, but rather populated with a diverse collection of *theoi* (gods), *daimones* (spirits), and other entities. I will try to cover all the major figures of Greek religion, but there are always more to learn about.

So first the gods we are most familiar with: Zeus, Hera, Ares, Poseidon, Apollon, Artemis, Demeter, Hephaistos, Athene, Aphrodite, Hermes and Dionysos. This is probably the most common list of "Olympians" although sometimes there are changes in the roll call, most notably Hestia present instead of Dionysos. We might think we know these gods from our childhood mythology books, but we would be wrong. Those books tend to portray the gods as almost caricatures, like the jealous wife Hera or the humiliated Hephaistos. But that is no more accurate than saying that I am an artist, period – it is only one aspect of myself.

To learn about the full complexity of a god, I suggest starting by reading all of their myths, and finding their various epithets. Epithets are cult titles that refer to the god's nature, traits, history, etc. They can often reveal an unexpected face of the god; for instance, Aphrodite has an epithet that means "bearing weapons," not something you might expect from the so-called "goddess of love." Some believe that epithets refer to different aspects of each god, but others (even in ancient times) treat those aspects as separate entities entirely. It is interesting to ponder, is Zeus Horkios (of oaths) absolutely the same being as Zeus Lukaios (of the wolf) or Zeus Meilikhios (gentle)?

It is also useful to learn all of the animals, plants, etc. that are associated with each god, or the gods in which you are interested (a list of some of these correspondences can be found in *Appendix II*). And even that would not be the end of it. In ancient times, offerings were left to gods for a variety of things, not always in keeping with their supposed "functions." Especially if the devotee had a previous relationship established with the god or goddess in question, they could be petitioned for almost anything.

Beyond the familiar Olympians, there are a few other gods and goddesses that are commonly worshipped, most notably (in my experience) but in no way limited to: Hekate, Asklepios, Helios, Selene, Pan and Eros.

A note about Hekate – this goddess is widely misunderstood by modern pagans (the same could be said about many of the Greek gods, but it is most common, I think, with Hekate). Because of her absorption into Wiccan practice and theology, many think she is either a "crone goddess" or even that she is a "maiden-mother-crone" archetype. However, in ancient Greek mythology, she is most often portrayed as a young woman, and her attributes and common devotions have little to do with the neo-pagan conception of her. Eros, too, is often misunderstood, mistaken for the Victorian winged cherub rather than the mature sexual force that he is. Let these examples remind you to take note of the background and bias of the sources you read, and always search for accurate depictions of the gods.

Hellenic religion is also full of groupings of gods and goddesses, usually in threes or multiples of three. There are the three Moirai, or Fates: Klotho, Lakhesis and Atropos. There are the three Horai, or

Seasons, and the three (sometimes four) Eumenides, or Kindly Ones, also known as the Furies (these latter are not really worshipped so much as they are stridently avoided). There are the nine Mousai, or Muses: Kalliope, Kleio, Euterpe, Terpsikhora, Erato, Melpomene, Thaleia, Poluhumnia, and Ourania, each with their own artistic specialty. And there are groups of male gods as well, such as the Kabeiroi, the Kouretes, etc. There are in fact so many of these groupings, sometimes of rather minor deities, that I couldn't list them all here. Only some of them are actively worshipped today, and this was true even in ancient times.

An important group of gods and spirits are called *khthonioi*, meaning of the underworld. These include Haides, Persephone, a few other chthonic divinities, and the souls of the dead (Hekate could also belong on this list, depending on your view of her, as could aspects of other gods such as Hermes Psychopompos). Haides is a god that is paid little cult, either today or in the past, mostly because he is dreaded, feared and respected more than he is loved. Persephone, on the other hand, was the center of the largest Mystery rites in ancient Greece, at Eleusis. Although she is only Queen of the Underworld for part of the year, it seems to be the aspect most attractive to worshippers.

The khthonioi are given rites somewhat differently than the other gods: they are offered black animals instead of white ones, they are worshipped primarily at night instead of during the day, sacrifices are made to them in a bothros (pit) instead of a raised bomos, their libations (khoai) are poured out in entirety, prayers are made to them with hands lowered instead of raised, and their holy places are caves and other underground places instead of temples.

## Ancestors

Like most polytheistic cultures, the ancient Greeks had rituals for honoring their ancestors. A family member who had died was still important, and deserved attention. These practices are beginning to grow again today, but since so many things have changed (funeral customs, the religions of our relatives), we must adapt without simply forgetting those who have come before us.

After the funerary rites (described in Chapter One) are over, the deceased relative is treated in much the same way as other chthonic beings. Food offerings and libations can be left at the gravesite, not only at the time of interment, but traditionally on certain days afterwards: the third, ninth and sometimes thirtieth days after the funeral, the deceased's birthday, the anniversary of the person's death, and community festivals honoring the dead (such as the ancient Athenian Genesia). In addition to food and drink left on the ground, ribbons and flowers can be left by the tomb. In ancient times, the oldest son of the family was the most obligated to pay respect to the ancestor, but everyone could be involved and in modern times it seems appropriate to share the responsibility equally among family members.

Ancestors were believed to give fertility of all kinds, and were often sacrificed to and prayed to for good crops and fertile wombs. However, the dead were also feared, and people would pass by graves silently, so as to avoid attracting the attention of the soul within. This custom, as well as the prevalence of rites performed at the graves themselves, shows that many people believed at least some aspect of the psyche remained in the grave site. When a person died away from home, their soul had to be called back somehow to an empty grave called a cenotaph, where the person was represented by a stone. Cenotaphs were tended by relatives in the same manner as real graves.

If you have deceased relatives who are buried nearby, of course the easiest way to continue these traditions would be to visit their graves at certain times and leave offerings. However, for those of us living further away, it seems appropriate to erect a small shrine in their honor, similar to the idea of a cenotaph, which can be the focus of our rituals. This shrine could include photographs of the deceased, objects once belonging to them, and other basic shrine elements such as an offering dish or incense (more on shrines later).

I think it is also appropriate to visit one's local cemetery and leave some libations to all the dead buried there. While I do not know of a precedent for this in ancient Greek custom (except for the Genesia, at which all the city's dead were honored), it seems appropriate to me to establish ties with the area you live in by honoring those who have lived there before, whose spirits (in some people's beliefs) would at least partially be linked to that part of the earth.

## Heroes

Another group often included in the khthonioi are the heroes. In ancient times, the heroes were men who had been (or were believed to have been) actual living people, worshipped after death as semi-divine. The cult of heroes was directly tied to their tombs (although sometimes many places would boast the tomb of the same hero), and their worship was closer to that of the dead than of the gods. They were offered the same types of foods and libations, and their shrines were passed in silence. A hero did not have to be of divine parentage, but was instead often honored for some exceptional quality or feat.

There were also cults of heroines in ancient Greece. Generally, the heroines were figures from mythology or poetry – such as Helen and Ariadne – rather than (supposedly) historical women. Sometimes, as is true with male heroes, it is difficult to draw the line between heroine and goddess, and some figures like Ino Leukothea were treated like one or the other in different locations.

While there were a few "pan-Hellenic" heroes (Herakles being the primary example of such), mostly this was a local phenomenon, each area having its own heroes. Therefore, when attempting to revive the worship of heroes in modern times, it seems less authentic to turn immediately to ancient Greek heroes, instead of identifying the heroes of our own culture and specific area. Such modern heroes are often the subjects of local folk songs and ballads (like the heroes of the *Iliad*), and are to some degree mythologized even when they began as real people – much in the way, I'm sure, that some ancient heroes were. There are sometimes even local variants of these modern hero legends, as there were in ancient times.

So how do we now pay cult to our local heroes? We can leave offerings at their graves (when possible) or at places associated with them. We can, as in ancient times, hold feasts in their honor. We can set aside a special day each year for them, or modify an existing civic holiday in their honor. We are not even committing much of an innovation in this, since as Burkert states, "Great gods are no longer born, but new heroes can always be raised up from the army of the dead whenever a family, cult association, or city passes an appropriate resolution to accord heroic honours." (*Greek Religion*, 206) Thus, recognizing new heroes and paying them cult is actually entirely within the structure of ancient Greek religion. And it is yet another way to bring the religion of the past fully into the present.

## The Nymphs

Worship of the nymphs – the divinities of the natural features of the landscape – was very important in ancient Greek religion, especially in the rural areas, and is now being slowly rediscovered. A shepherd or farmer in ancient Greece might have paid more regular cult to the nymphs than he would to the Olympians, because the nymphs impacted his daily life. They lived all around him in the woods, in his pastures, they guarded the spring water his goats drank, they lived in the same caves that gave him occasional shelter. Greek pastoral poetry even speaks of shepherds meeting and sometimes falling in love with nymphs, during the long hours they spent with their flocks on mountainsides.

There are many different names for the nymphs, depending on what type they are. The word nymph (*numphe* in Greek) itself means "bride," although nymphs are rarely married; however they are always female – their male counterparts are the satyrs, silens, and kentaurs. Dryads are nymphs of the trees, especially oaks, who are so bound together that they are born and die with their trees. (In general, nymphs are said to live extremely long lives, but are not actually immortal.) Oreads are nymphs of the mountains. Naiads belong to springs and other bodies of water, whereas nereids are nymphs of the ocean, and limnades live in lakes, marshes and swamps. Epimeliades protect sheep flocks, and leimoniades reside in flowery meadows. There are many more.

Some individual nymphs figure prominently in mythology: Thetis (a nereid), the mother of Akhilles; Echo who fled from Pan; Daphne who was chased by Apollon and became his beloved laurel tree; and Maia, the mother of Hermes. In myths, the nymphs are most often in the company of (or being chased by) Pan, Hermes, Apollon and Dionysos – the rural or pastoral gods. Whereas mythology tends to portray these relationships as rather unwelcome or hostile, in cult it seems these gods were worshipped side by side with the nymphs, with no animosity suggested. An example of such were the nymphs of the Korykian Cave on Mount Parnassos, above sacred Delphi. This cave was particularly holy, not just to the nymphs but to Pan, Hermes and perhaps Dionysos as well. The nymphs there are mentioned in the *Homeric Hymn to Hermes*, when Apollon tells Hermes to find them, for they will teach him the skills of divination. They are portrayed as bees, and in fact the nymphs were often associated with bees elsewhere, and honey is known as an especially appropriate gift for them.

Almost everywhere, the nymphs were known for their healing abilities (also often present in the waters they protect) and for their prophetic powers. Religious rites for them often included some form of simple divination, like the use of *astragaloi* (sheep knucklebones). Thousands of knucklebones were found in the archaeological excavation of the Korykian Cave, and of many other nymph caves in

Greece. The nymphs can also bestow this gift of prophecy on certain mortals; such a person might then become a nympholept. The word nympholepsy has a number of connotations. One refers to an overall heightened awareness and increased verbal skills, also a gift from the nymphs, which makes a man into a poet. A more negative version of nympholepsy views possession by the nymphs as an unwanted illness. Sometimes the word describes a physical rapture, an actual abduction of a person by the nymphs. Finally, a nympholept can mean a person who is exceptionally devoted in a religious sense to the nymphs, one who keeps a sanctuary for them and is inspired to prophesize. Historically, these nympholepts occupied a marginalized role in society like many other visionary types, and yet they often created and maintained important cult sites for the nymphs that were visited by pilgrims. The nympholept sometimes had a special relationship with one particular nymph, a relationship that may have been romantic and/or sexual in nature.

The love of the nymphs was so strong in the Greek people that it survived the conversion to Christianity, and is the one major feature of ancient religion still practiced up to recent times. In modern rural Greece, all nymphs are now called nereids, but the myths and practices have stayed relatively unchanged over the centuries. Tales are still told of boys or men being captured by a nymph, and offerings are still made at wells and rivers and such. As Nilsson writes, the worship of local nature spirits "was the most persistent....form of Greek religion." (*Greek Folk Religion*, 18)

However, modern Hellenic paganism has, up until recently, largely overlooked this important aspect of ancient practice; we have focused overly much on the "major" gods and the cult of the city. Yet the nymphs are present everywhere, even in cities. In Athens there were still places to worship the nymphs, usually around wells. And so there are fountains, and trees, and parks in our modern cities, plenty of places to feel the presence of the nymphs and pay them cult. It is easy to begin, just leave offerings in your area at a prominent river or stream, a beautiful tree, cave, or any other natural feature. You might also consider the spirits of natural features that share a name with the town or county you live in to be the patron nymphs of your area, in the way that Athens was named after Athene (for instance, the Great Salt Lake's nymph would be special to Salt Lake City residents).

Another way to find remarkable nymphs is to research the places that were traditionally considered sacred by the indigenous peoples of your area and visit them with the intention of creating bonds with the spirits that reside there. The polytheists that originally lived in the United States were the Native American tribes, so it makes sense to find out what places they believed to be sacred, what gods they had, etc. After all, when the Greeks went to Egypt, they didn't just make up a whole new set of religious places and figures there, they adopted the Egyptian ones, and combined some of them with their own. They would have listened to an Egyptian who told them a particular place was sacred, or that such-and-such river had a strong deity present. I'm not suggesting that we take up Native American religion, but why start from scratch if you can find a local pagan history to begin with?

Appropriate offerings to the nymphs include libations (some will say that only wineless libations are appropriate, but Van Straten makes a good argument that wine was indeed offered to the nymphs in some areas), astragaloi, honey, jewelry, shells, and votive female figurines. You could also build a shrine in the wilds, to honor them.

One of my favorite ways to interact with the nymphs is to hold a *theoxenia* for them. A theoxenia is a feast held in honor of a god or gods, to which the deity is invited and served as a special guest – essentially a divine dinner party (for more information on this ritual, I recommend Michael Jameson's article in *Ancient Greek Cult Practice From the Epigraphical Evidence*). A formal invitation is made for the god. Tables are set opulently, food and drink served, music played. Sometimes there is an object, such as a small statue, at one seat to represent the god. The god's plate is heaped high with good food, his/her cup filled with wine, and the god's presence is felt throughout the meal.

Adapting a theoxenia festival for the nymphs would not be breaking new ground. We know that there was one held for Dionysos and the nymphs at Mytilene, called the Theodaisia. And banquets in general were considered appropriate offerings for them. But I suggest that a particularly appropriate format for a nymph theoxenia would be as an outdoor picnic.

The first step is to find a nymph-haunted place in your area. This might be an especially beautiful spot, or one where you feel inspired. It might be a prominent natural feature, such as the largest river or mountain nearby. If hosting a theoxenia for a particular type of nymph, you would need to search out their specific home – for instance, a marshy place for the limnades, a riverbank for the naiads. Before the meal (or even a couple days before) it might be a good idea to clean up the area if there is litter – not only is this a good gesture towards the nymphs of the place, but beautifying natural areas was actually a form of devotional activity for the nymphs in ancient times too.

I like to make physical invitations, such as handmade cards for the nymphs for my theoxenia. Afterwards, they can be burnt as offerings, left on my indoor shrine, or saved with other mementos. A beautiful space can be created for the meal on the spot chosen, using a nice picnic blanket, actual plates and cups (rather than paper or plastic), flowers, and other decorations. A full place setting should be laid out for the nymphs, including silverware, napkin, etc., and obviously also a full portion of the food and drink that is served. The menu should include something they might particularly like, such as honeybuns or strawberry shortcake. Pure spring water would make both a good drink and libation liquid, as might mead (honey-wine).

I begin the festival with a libation and the reading of a hymn or prayer; my favorite is the Orphic Hymn to the Nymphs, which mentions several different types. Reading the invitation out loud is a nice gesture as well. I would also suggest that during the meal, irrelevant conversation be kept to a minimum, and the guests should be aware of the presence of the nymphs around them, and act accordingly. Poetry could be read, songs sung, instruments played. Music and dance are especially pleasing to the nymphs. When everyone is ready to go home, a final libation should be poured, and the nymphs should be thanked for being guests. Make sure not to leave any litter behind; the spot should look just as good or better than when you came. Finally, coming back to the same place repeatedly for future nymph picnics would be a good way to establish kharis with the local nymphs.

I think that some people, having endeavored to meet and spend time with the nymphs in their area, might even develop a more personal and intimate relationship with a specific nymph, along the lines of the ancient nympholepts (more on them in the next chapter).

## Other Spirits

There are other nature spirits besides the nymphs. As I mentioned before, the male counterparts to the nymphs were such beings as the satyrs (part man, part horse or goat) and kentaurs (half man, half horse), although there is little evidence of them being paid cult in ancient times. However, the god Pan, also half goat, was widely worshipped, especially in his homeland of Arkadia, but also everywhere in forests and other wild places. He can be worshipped today both in the same manner as other gods, and/or as the nymphs are.

Another group of figures that are both gods and directly tied to the natural landscape are the river gods. Often depicted as bulls with human heads, or as having bull's horns, the river gods are the fathers of the river nymphs (sometimes called potamiads or okeanids), and control the flow of the river itself.

The spirits of the winds are called the Anemoi; the most well-known are Boreas (north), Notos (south), Apheliotes (east) and Zephuros (west). Some evidence has been found that the Anemoi were worshipped with regular cult, but little detail is known.

Most of these figures could be called *daimones*, a word which usually refers to a type of spiritual being that is a little less powerful and wide-reaching than a god (although sometimes *daimon* and *theos* are used interchangeably). Over the centuries, this word gained an entirely negative connotation (later morphing into our word demon), but it was originally a more neutral term that could encompass both beneficent and malevolent spirits.

## Agathos Daimon

One of the most important concepts in Greek religion is the Agathos Daimon (also called agathodaimon), which translates roughly as "good spirit." The Agathos Daimon is a spirit of fortune and good luck. It can belong to and protect an entire household, and as such it receives libations of wine after meals. It can sometimes be seen around the house in the form of a snake.

Originally an androgynous being, in Hellenistic times the Agathos Daimon became decidedly male, and was even said to be the consort of Agathe Tukhe, the goddess of fortune. It was portrayed as a young man holding a cornucopia. Yet it still retained its serpentine form, for when a huge snake appeared to Alexander at the future site of Alexandria and then was killed, he erected a hero shrine for it as the Agathos Daimon.

The tradition of the Agathos Daimon seems to exist on a more individual level than the rites of the gods or even heroes. There were no large festivals for this spirit, no hymns that I know of. In Boiotia, the opening of new wine jars was dedicated to the Agathos Daimon, but that is the only reference to it in the realm of public festival. While the second day of each month was set aside for worship of the Agathos Daimon (in the ancient Athenian calendar), it seems that was a more private affair, the actions of a household or individual rather than a community.

One could almost call the Agathos Daimon a sort of guardian angel, attached to a person at birth to protect and guide him or her throughout life. It also affects an individual's luck. Sokrates said that his told him when to stop or keep quiet. It was thought that one needed to appease one's Agathos Daimon so that it would respond favorably. Pindar wrote, "The daimon active about me I will always consciously put to rights with me by cultivating him according to my means."

The daimones stand between gods and men, they are as Plato said the "interpreters and ferrymen." Much in the way Vodounists believe in the Christian god but prefer to have interactions with the *lwa*, the daimones are in some ways closer, more accessible than the gods. A relationship with a daimon can be very personal and intimate; it is also a bridge to relationships with the gods. As Pindar said, "The great mind of Zeus steers the daimon of the men whom he loves."

The Agathos Daimon is part of a widespread history of personal spirits in polytheistic religions around the world. The Romans called it a Genius, and in Slavic folklore it was a Dola (a personal fate and protective spirit). It is very similar to the fylgja of Norse tradition. And yet, many Hellenic polytheists largely ignore daimones in general, and few acknowledge their own Agathos Daimon. I think adopting this ancient tradition will add something to our religion. I think it will encourage the possibility of intimate spiritual relationships with divine entities, and even bring us closer to the gods. I also see it as an opportunity to integrate our practice with the world in which we live. The actual spirit who belongs to you (and to whom you belong) will probably be tied to your family, and/or the land around you, and relating to it in the context of Greek religious practice brings our religion fully into the present time and place.

You can begin a relationship with your Agathos Daimon by saving out the second day of the month for it, leaving libations, and spending some time trying to get a feel for it. When you have an extraordinary piece of luck, you might thank your Agathos Daimon in some way. When you need guidance, you might turn first to it before asking the gods. Your Agathos Daimon can be an invaluable teacher, protector and guide, and I also believe that the tradition can encompass a romantic and/or sexual way of relating to this spirit, much in the same vein as the nympholepts.

## Household Religion

The Agathos Daimon is also a part of the private household cult – those daily practices centered in and around the house – which was and is an important aspect of Greek religion. After meals, a few drops of unmixed wine would be poured out onto the floor for the Agathos Daimon, often perceived here as a snake. While we no longer have earthen floors to absorb libations, we can still pour out this drink into a small dish, and periodically dispose of the offerings outside on the ground.

First and foremost in the household is Hestia. She is less anthropomorphized than the rest of the Greek gods, rather she *is* the hearth itself. In an ancient house, the hearth occupied a central place, and was the focus of virtually all private sacrifices and offerings. Meals were eaten around the hearth, and at the beginning of any meal a portion would be dropped in the fire for Hestia. She was also the first to receive a piece of a sacrifice made in the home. There is evidence that this led to Hestia being recognized first in larger public sacrifices as well. Any new member of the family was first brought to the hearth, people even swore oaths on the hearth.

Of course, modern homes rarely have a fireplace; we certainly do not tend to use them for daily cooking. Hellenic pagans have come up with a variety of solutions to this. Some consider their kitchen stove to be their hearth, especially if it is gas powered and therefore has a flame. In this case, a piece of the meal might be put into the oven or burned on the stovetop. Others opt to have a candle or oil lamp lit for Hestia in the kitchen, (although it is unsafe to leave it burning while asleep or away).

The storeroom, or pantry, is protected by Zeus Ktesios (acquirer). In fact, many of Zeus' lesser-known aspects are involved in the household cult. Traditionally, a jar or amphora is dedicated to Zeus Ktesios and placed in the storeroom; it is filled with fresh water, oil, and various fruits (a panspermia type of offering) and the handles are decorated with wool fillets. This Zeus, like the Agathos Daimon, often takes the form of a snake. (In fact, not only is the belief in a snake house-spirit prevalent across European paganism, it could even still be found in rural areas of Greece well into the last century.) The jar for Zeus Ktesios is a fairly simple offering to assemble, and can be placed in modern pantries or just on the shelves you use for foodstuffs.

The rest of the household religion could be found immediately outside the doors of any ancient Greek person's house. Here again we find Zeus; an altar to Zeus Herkeios (fence) stood in the courtyard and received sacrifices and libations. Some houses also erected an altar to Zeus Kataibates (who descends) in front of their houses to protect them from lightning strikes. Further, where the courtyard met the street, might stand a high, conical stone in honor of Apollon Aguieos (of the street). Oil was poured on it, and it was decorated with fillets; it stood to protect the house against harm. In front of the house one might also find Hermes Propulaios (before the gates) in the shape of a pillar, or a triple image of Hekate. Prayers would be made to these for protection and to avert evil.

Aside from replicating these altars and stones exactly, which many of us cannot do, there are ways to carry on these traditions even in an apartment. An image of one or all of these protecting gods could be hung on the front door (inside, if outside is not possible), or perhaps a pile of stones placed by the front step where one could pour libations. Considering what a large part of the average person's religious life these small rituals would have occupied in ancient Greece, it seems only proper that we continue to perform them today, if slightly modified. And it is always a good idea to incur the good-will of the gods when it comes to your family and home.

## Shrines

It is also appropriate to have other shrines set up in addition to those for the household. It is true that "Greek houses had no separate room for a household shrine and rarely had special permanent altars." (Price, 89) However, it is also true that in ancient Greece there were large temples everywhere, and statues in the streets, and a person didn't usually have to go far to reach some sort of shrine. I think that considering our present circumstances, with most of us spread out across the country and even the world, it makes sense to tend to small shrines in our houses if we choose.

Hellenic pagan shrines (I often avoid the word altar as it has too many connotations not applicable to this context) can be simple or extravagant. There are not many rules, there is no common layout like Wiccan altars have. Generally, a shrine is dedicated to a single god, goddess or daimon, but it is still in keeping with tradition to have more than one god honored at the same place, especially if there are space concerns. You can build a shrine as big or small as you want, or as your living space allows. Bureau tops, end tables, nightstands, bookshelves, coffee tables, plaster pillars from the craft store, all of these will suffice. You can have one big shrine, a bunch of smaller ones, or anything in between.

An average Hellenic shrine might have a cult image (statue, painting, etc) of the god/dess, an offering bowl, a candle (the ancient Greeks used oil lamps, and we can do that today, but most people find candles easier to find and to manage), incense, and small libation jugs for water, wine, etc. It might also be home to permanent offerings made by the worshipper (perhaps a small ceramic dolphin for Apollon, for instance). The most important things to have are implements of basic ritual, and items that remind you of the god(s) involved. Those who do not confine their worship primarily to one or several deities might wish to set up a shrine to all the gods, or the Olympian gods, or something like that. Considering that there was a shrine to "the Twelve Gods" in the ancient Agora of Athens, this seems appropriate too.

When you first build your shrine, you should start by sprinkling khernips (pure water) over the base and every object that will be on it. Then I recommend lighting a candle or oil lamp and perhaps some incense, and making an initial sacrifice to ask the gods' blessing for the shrine. Especially if it is dedicated to one particular god, you might want to invite the god to reside (partially, of course) within that space, in the same way that an ancient temple was the home of the god.

Make sure that your shrines are in a safe place where nothing will be knocked over. And be sure to keep them clean – regularly clear away old offerings, wash out bowls and cups used for libations, and dust everything off once in awhile too. I personally think it's a good idea to completely disassemble, clean, and reassemble your shrines at least once a year (perhaps for the ancient, or modern, new year). Tending a shrine, performing ritual there and putting work into it, adding objects and clearing away old ones, is a very satisfying ongoing devotional act. It is not necessary, but I think the effort is appreciated by the gods, and it also gives one a special place at which to connect to the gods.

It is also possible to make small, portable shrines to carry with you while traveling (or to keep primarily at your house if you don't have much space). A small box can be decorated and filled with miniature versions of all the normal shrine objects. However, remember that Hellenic practice can be carried out anywhere without special items. If you are away from your residence, you can still make libations, pray, and perform other acts of devotion. A bottle of juice bought at a convenience store and poured out on a patch of ground is a sufficient libation. Leaving a coin at a crossroads in the middle of a city is an offering to Hermes. You can say a morning prayer no matter where you wake up. Reminders of the gods are everywhere.

You can also create shrines in natural places, in the woods or fields or parks. Even if you do not own land, there are ways to make unobtrusive gifts to the gods, or to create a *temenos* (a place set apart, dedicated to the gods). These can be temporary or even made permanent. In ancient times, "one could hardly have taken a step out of doors without meeting a little shrine, a sacred enclosure, an image, a sacred stone, or a sacred tree." (Nilsson, *Greek Folk Religion*, 18) You can start to build such a network of sacred places in your own area slowly: a heap of stones for Hermes, a stream at which you regularly leave flowers for the nymphs, a lightning-struck tree on which you carve a prayer to Zeus.

## Holy Places

"In antiquity sanctity was inherent in the place. The place was not made holy by building a house for a god on it, but a house for a god was built on a certain place because the place was holy." (Nilsson, *Greek Folk Religion*, 76) So how do you identify especially sacred places? There are a few ways. One is to notice prominent natural features, such as the tallest mountain or largest river around, or particularly breathtaking ones. "Anything which gave the impression of singular beauty and strength appeared at once to the Greeks to be impregnated with the divine." (Festugiere, 9) Or, as I mentioned in the discussion on nymphs, anything sharing a name with the town/county/area you live in, as well as areas considered sacred by indigenous peoples, or otherwise possessing a history of being valued spiritually.

The gods are said to favor certain places in Greece – Aphrodite has Kupros, Apollon has Delos, Athene of course has Athens, etc. We do not know if the gods will begin to develop ties to any special areas where we currently worship them, but I would not rule out the possibility. It might be worthwhile as our religion develops to occasionally perform divinations or look for omens regarding this matter. It would be wonderful to have places of pilgrimage in our own countries.

## Prayer

I've spoken of sacred places, created both by nature and by our own hands, and of the offerings made there, but what words are spoken to accompany these actions? Well, the most basic acts of worship can be carried out without words, and certainly without any fancy formulae or ritual scripts. If you wish to say something, it can merely be "for Hera" as a libation is poured, or the greeting *"khaire"* (*"khairete"* if you are addressing more than one deity) to the image(s) on your shrine as you pass. A more eloquent dedication might be "to the beautiful nymphs who reside in these waters, may this gift please you" or something of the sort. These small gestures can be expressed in extemporaneous words. However, for formal ritual, or for important requests or thanksgivings, a traditional prayer is appropriate.

"[P]rayer for a Greek meant asking the gods for something. One had to give as well as take. One did not customarily approach the gods empty handed. Prayer was not of itself an autonomous mode of religious action. It relied on sacrifice." (Pulleyn, 15) This is crucial: an offering must be made or at least promised if you are asking for something (and never neglect to fulfill your promises to the gods!) and often also if you are giving thanks. If you wish merely to voice your praise and love for the god/dess, a hymn is more appropriate, which is after all an offering in itself.

It is customary when praying to the "heavenly" gods to stand with arms stretched upwards. For the gods of the sea, the arms are stretched out ahead of you, and for the khthonioi the arms are pointed downward (though in particularly emotional prayers to the khthonioi sometimes the person would fall to the ground and beat their hands upon it). Prayers are spoken out loud, unless this is impossible for some reason. "The gods, of course, can also hear soft entreaties; and in exceptional cases, in the cult of the uncanny, subterranean gods, silent prayer is prescribed." (Burkert, 73) Generally, a prayer (like a hymn) is addressed to only one god or goddess at a time, although there can be exceptions to this rule.

First, the worshipper calls to the god: "hear me" or "come" are common openings. (For words and prayers in Greek, see *Appendix III*.) Then the god is addressed by name; in Greek this takes the vocative case. It is also customary to name a few of the god's epithets (these can even replace the proper name entirely), and sometimes the formula "or by whatever name it pleases you to be called" is added. One might then speak of the places they are known to dwell, their birth place or famous temple sites; often the god is asked to come from whatever place he or she currently is. If the worshipper has previously sacrificed to this god, or the god has assisted them in the past, these instances are mentioned. Then finally a request is made, accompanied by a vow to sacrifice to the god if the prayer is answered (if the sacrifice has not already been made as an encouragement for the desired outcome).

One of the most famous prayers from ancient literature is that of Khruses, a priest of Apollon, in the opening stanzas of the *Iliad*. "'Hear me,' he cried, 'O god of the silver bow, you who protect Khruse and holy Killa and rule Tenedos with your might, hear me Sminthian god. If ever I have decked your temple with garlands, or burned for you thigh-bones in fat of bulls or goats, grant my prayer, and let your arrows avenge these my tears upon the Danaans.'" This example includes most of the elements I have outlined, and should give you an idea of how a complete prayer sounds.

With some practice and repetition, this format will become fairly easy to apply to any type of prayer you wish to make, to any god. You can add to it, make it more elaborate, or keep it to the bare bones. In time you can find a style, while still keeping within the tradition, that feels right to you and complements the relationships you have with the gods.

You might wish to forget about this formulaic type of prayer and simply speak from your heart. I cannot say that it is altogether bad or wrong to talk to the gods informally at times, or to communicate with them intuitively; that can be fruitful. However, there is also a place for formal entreaty. These are still gods, after all. It is wise to take the warning offered by C.S. Lewis in *The Screwtape Letters* (although this was directed at Christians, it can still apply to us): "In reaction against [formal, institutionalized prayer], he may be persuaded to aim at something entirely spontaneous, inward, informal, and unregularised; and what this will actually mean to a beginner will be an effort to produce in himself a vaguely devotional *mood* in which real concentration of will and intelligence have no part." The gods deserve our best efforts, and a true outreaching, not simply a satisfied feeling on our parts.

Some people are concerned that their prayers may be seen as too superficial or unimportant by the gods. Is it okay to pray for a new job or a girlfriend or to win your baseball game? I certainly think so. I don't see why it should be considered superficial to ask the gods for things we need, or even just things we want. As long as the proper form is followed, as long as we make offerings along with our requests, and as long as we don't start *expecting* things from them, it seems perfectly appropriate to me. And certainly in keeping with tradition, since the ancient Greeks had no problems praying for whatever they wanted, even the destruction of their enemies! I once prayed to Hermes quite strongly for a financial windfall – I was barely scraping by – and he delivered. I spent a lot of that money on offerings, of course, and a pilgrimage to Greece. I didn't get the sense from him that he was offended by the secular nature of my request – I am after all a physical person with physical wants and needs.

One final thought regarding prayers – it has become popular in pagan circles recently to create prayer beads for various gods, themes, or needs. While there is no tradition of prayer beads within Hellenismos, I see no reason why they shouldn't be included either. A string of prayer beads could include representations of each god you are involved with, or even various aspects of a single god. You can design formal prayers to be spoken with the beads, or use them as a vehicle or inspiration to talking with your gods more personally, pausing at each bead to acknowledge the deity it represents in some way – with a request, gratitude, praise, etc. Prayer beads can also become a sort of portable shrine, and a way to take your religious practice with you whenever you travel. And they are an excellent way to begin, or enhance, a daily spiritual practice.

## Listening to the Gods

Prayer is how we speak to the gods. But how do they speak to us? Some might say that it is hubris to think the gods speak to us at all, but in my opinion the most rewarding part of Hellenic polytheism is establishing a reciprocal relationship with the gods – and reciprocal means *both ways*. Letting the gods communicate to you can be an active or passive process, but it always means paying attention to how they might be interacting with you in your life. Just like getting that new job you wanted should prompt you to thank Hermes, other more subtle things in your life might be at least partly due to the gods. This doesn't mean that every little thing, good or bad, is cause to think a god is involved, but you should be open to the possibility.

The most common way of ascertaining the will of the gods, asking them questions, or just generally trying to get a grasp on a situation, is divination. "Divination was a primary means of bridging the gap between the known and the unknown, the visible and the invisible, the past and the future, and the human and the divine....Divination was so vitally important to the Greeks that it was included, second only to medicine, among the *technai* (arts, skills, or crafts) that Prometheus gave to humankind." (Flower, 8)

Divination does not necessarily mean fortune-telling; despite the common misconception, it is not primarily used for seeing the future. Rather, it gives one insight into the inner mechanism of life itself, of fate, it shows us where we are, what is going on around us. It is also a tool to help us understand what the gods might want to tell us. As such, remember that it should be treated respectfully, that the process should be undertaken – when possible – in a spiritual manner, after making offerings and prayers, and with an open mind.

I also think that it is best if divination is performed in a light meditative state. The actual mechanism of divination is not really the cards or dice or whatever, but a communication from the divine world to ours. The tools make it easier, but so does the right state of mind. Emptying your thoughts and making your mind receptive to that communication will increase your chances of performing a useful divination. Insights and epiphanies do not usually come to a cluttered and distracted mind.

### Divination Methods

According to my survey, and my own experience, many Hellenic polytheists use non-Hellenic methods of divination at least some of the time, and often more than they use ancient Greek ones. This is, I think, perfectly acceptable – after all, if the ancient Greeks were still around today, they certainly might adopt some new forms of divination as they became exposed to them, in the same way as they did occasionally in ancient times. Therefore Tarot, scrying, and other methods from various cultures and even our modern society can all be used in a Hellenic context, although I recommend really becoming familiar with a divination system and learning about its own context before applying it to Hellenic practice. (The only exception I might make here is the Norse runes, which are more than just a divination tool and are often misunderstood by people outside of that religious and magical system.)

That being said, there are also quite a few ancient Greek divinatory methods that can still be used today. At most ancient sacrifices, the animal was examined after it was cut open, and certain aspects of its anatomy were viewed as divinatory objects, most often the liver. There is a whole complicated method to this procedure, called haruspicy, but since most people are not in the position to perform it today, it is largely ignored.

Something we can do today, and rather easily, is ornithomancy, or divination by birds. There were probably more rules to this practice in ancient times than we know of today, but some basics are as follows: a bird from the West (or left) is seen as negative or bad, a bird from the East (or right) is positive or good. Generally birds of prey are much more significant than other birds. Anything unusual or noticeable can be a sign – their flight speed, noises they make, sudden changes in direction, etc. You can also set up a system whereby you define certain activities as meaning certain things, and then see which happen. Overall, this is a divinatory system that is wide open to interpretation and personal intuition.

On the opposite end of the spectrum, there are some systems that are fairly straightforward, or at least give you some words on which to base your interpretation. The Homeric Oracle is one example; it can be found in the *Greek Magical Papyri* which is a set of magical and religious documents dating primarily to the Hellenistic period in Egypt, when Greek and Egyptian cultures blended to a degree. It is used by rolling three dice, and the three-number combination that results is used to look up a particular line from either the *Iliad* or *Odyssey*. If you cannot find the original text for this, you should note that this is basically a form of bibliomancy, and could just as easily be performed by randomly opening one of these books and pointing to a line, which then becomes your oracle. It is important when using this type of system to ask a clear, simple question before divining, since otherwise the answer will not be as easy to apply.

Another ancient system that some Hellenic polytheists use is called the Limyran Oracle – it consists of twenty-four sentences, each connected to a letter of the Greek alphabet. A group of stones or potsherds is each inscribed with one letter, and then one is chosen – the corresponding sentence is your oracle. More information on this oracle can be found on a website listed under Internet Resources at the end of this book.

One of the simplest and most common forms of ancient Greek divination was kleromancy, or divination by lots. This could take many forms, using knucklebones, stones, or any other small object. The lots were thrown on the ground, and the resulting patterns were examined and interpreted to find an answer to the question or problem. While we don't know much specific information on how this was done, any system of meanings attributed to the patterns can work, as long as you stick to it – otherwise the divination is meaningless.

The same is true for oneiromancy, or divination through dreams. There are plenty of modern books on dream symbolism available, but most generalize a bit too much – dreams are personal, and even if sometimes you might tap into what Jung called the "collective unconscious" and dream of symbols that are universally meaningful, a lot of what happens in your dreams will have special significance to you that it wouldn't have to anyone else. So develop a knowledge of both universal and personal systems and then stick with it when you examine your dreams.

In ancient times, dreams were used especially for healing, and there were multiple sanctuaries where people could go to do ritual and make sacrifice, then sleep in a special place and wait for a dream wherein the god would either heal them or give them information that would lead to a cure in waking life – this is called dream incubation, and the most famous of these sites was Epidauros. It is entirely possible to do something similar today, using the basic forms of ritual and prayer, provided you have a private, quiet place to sleep afterwards. Remember that if you are cured, you must leave a thanks-offering to the god (or goddess, technically any god might choose to help you, although traditionally it was Asklepios who was petitioned in these matters) – frequently this took the form of a plaque or other image of the body part that was healed, but other offerings are appropriate as well.

A whole separate category of divination is direct inspiration – this differs from deductive divination in that it does not utilize tools (at least as its main method) but relies on the contact between human and god. Usually an intense working relationship has to be developed between *mantis* and god for this to be effective. It is not something done lightly, or by everyone. I will discuss this further, particularly the tradition of the Pythia, in the next chapter.

When performing divination, it can sometimes be difficult to discern how much one's own interests are affecting one's interpretations. In other words, do the cards appear to say what they do because they are truly revealing the gods' communication, or are you just seeing what you want to see? A good way to insure against too much bias on your part is to check for confirmatory omens afterwards. This means keeping an eye out for signs that might confirm (or deny) what you read in your divination – not just repeating a divination for the same question. So, for instance, if your divination indicated that you should be making sacrifices to Poseidon more often, and the next day you meet a sailor for the first time, that's a helpful confirmation.

## Omens

Omens are another way of discovering what the gods wish to tell you; they can also be warnings, or even just indications of a divine presence around you. "The Athenians, like most peoples, felt the presence of their deities in significant events they found to be mysterious and inexplicable." (Mikalson, 17) Omens are also found in what might seem to be rather mundane occurrences.

"The god-sent sign is the instrument of mediation between the knowledge of the gods and the more limited knowledge of humans....it was also essential first to recognize the sign as a sign. A chance event becomes an omen when the circumstances require it, 'when the underlying tension of a personal situation kindles the signifying power of an omen.' The meaning of some omens and portents was obvious once they were recognized as such, of others less so; but in either case there could be no interpretation until the act of recognition had taken place." (Flower, 73)

Some people are skeptical about interpreting anything as an omen, especially if it seems to make a person look egotistical, like they believe everything that happens is a sign meant for them. Certainly, one doesn't want to over-interpret every single thing; but that doesn't mean that omens can't exist. Events can have material and divine explanations at the same time. For instance, if you ask Zeus for a response to something, and a lightning storm happens shortly afterwards, that can be taken as an omen – but it does not mean that the storm happened only for you, or would not have happened otherwise. Perhaps it came a little sooner or closer to you than it would have in order to serve as your sign. Perhaps it was Zeus who put it into your head to ask for a sign in the first place, knowing that the storm was coming.

Some of the most common categories of omen are rather mundane and simple – what makes them omens is the context in which they happen and how they are viewed by the person involved. Even sneezes and twitches were seen as potential omens in ancient Greece. As for how to interpret these, while sometimes they can just be a call to pay attention or a confirmation of something just said, "the primary significance attached to involuntary motions of the body [follows] the natural associations of the part affected," e.g., a tingling of the hand signifies money coming, something involving the ear portends hearing news, etc. (Halliday, 177)

One form of omen, called the *kledon*, can happen anywhere – it is a snatch of overheard conversation, even a single word, that seems to answer a question or problem you were having when you heard it. In ancient times this was even turned into a more elaborate type of divination sacred to Hermes: the querent goes to a marketplace, lights a lamp at a statue of Hermes, leaves a coin, presents his or her question, then walks into the crowd with ears covered. Once in the middle of the marketplace, the querent uncovers his or her ears and takes the first words heard as the omen. This can easily be done today at any supermarket, shopping mall, or ideally an outdoors farmers or crafts market. While we do not have statues of Hermes present in these places today, you can either bring an image of Hermes, or perform the ritual at a crossroads which is sacred to him. Leave a coin, light incense or a candle if you can, even for a moment, and then ask your question and leave the rest to Hermes.

Another type of omen also related to Hermes are the *enodioi sumboloi*: chance meetings on the road. Traveling, especially by foot, was an exhausting and sometimes even dangerous activity in ancient times. Portents were often looked for along the way. One such sign would be an encounter with another person, who might by his appearance, occupation, words, or some other aspect become meaningful to the traveler. We embark on journeys all the time even today, and especially on important travels one should be aware of possible omens like this. At home, one could still receive messages from the gods through an *oikoskopikon* – an incident of domestic life with import for the person involved. I have not found any examples of what this might entail, but if you keep an open mind and open eye, one might present itself to you if the gods wish it.

## Patron Gods

Many Hellenic polytheists direct their practice toward the gods in general, a large group of gods, or whatever deity seems appropriate at the time (e.g. leaving an offering one week for Aphrodite to thank her for a new relationship, the next week pouring a libation to Hermes to ask for protection on a journey). However, some people are drawn to one god or goddess (or a few) more than the rest, and feel called to devote themselves to that deity in a special way – not forsaking the other gods, but not worshipping them as frequently or as passionately. This relationship is commonly called having a patron god. "The god to whom a man entrusts himself is his god by choice; and the very fact of his choice is proof of a personal religion, which can lead to a more intimate bond than would otherwise exist between the chosen god and his worshipper." (Festugiere, 40)

There has been some debate on whether or not the concept of a patron god is a modern innovation. Some see it as mere mimicry of Wicca and other neopagan paths. Others compare it to the patron saint relationship in Catholicism. However, I think this concept was present in ancient Greece, although perhaps not as common as in modern times. It is said, for instance, that the famous playwright Aiskhulos had a dream of Dionysos as a boy, while lying in a vineyard, in which the god told him to write tragedies (Pausanias I, 59). Aiskhulos indeed spent the rest of his life in service to the god of theatre. In the *Odyssey*, it is clear that Odysseus has a special relationship with Athene; she counsels him and favors him above others, and he returns her devotion. The poet Sappho was a servant of Aphrodite. Certain priests volunteered for their positions, and it is reasonable to assume that some of them did so out of special love for the god or goddess of that temple. A perusal of the votive inscriptions we have from antiquity will show the depth of love, gratitude and even friendship possible on the part of the giver – some even allude to an established relationship between worshipper and god.

I would also venture to say that even if the patron relationship was extremely rare in ancient Greece, it is a worthwhile pursuit today, when so many of us feel called by a certain god. Perhaps with so few worshippers these days, the gods are more likely to pay individual attention to us. Perhaps, since we are all essentially converts, we are more likely to develop a passionate love for a god or gods than in the days when it was the established religion. Whatever the reasons behind it, I would think it foolish to ignore the attention of any of the gods. Now, some people have no interest in having a patron or simply never develop that relationship, which is perfectly acceptable too. It is not necessary for a meaningful Hellenic polytheist practice. But for those who do have a patron or patrons, it is an experience unlike any other.

In general, I would caution against just picking a god or goddess and calling them your patron. There are gods that are patrons of certain professions, roles, groups (even families and cities in ancient times), so for example if you are a blacksmith you could say your professional patron is Hephaistos. But that is not the same thing as a personal patron. Even if you do choose a god because you like what you know of their myths, attributes, etc., you might find that a deeper relationship never develops – after all, if you chose your mate based on his or her appearance or job, it might not work out. Developing a real relationship with a god is like falling in love, it transcends all the superficial ideas and desires and gets to the heart of things. You might even be surprised at who your patron turns out to be, if you indeed have one.

A patron relationship can take many forms. Some people relate to their patron as mother or father, sister or brother, friend, guide or counselor, even lover or husband or wife – sometimes even a combination of them all. Whatever the case, it is a bond as strong as any of those human relationships, and often even deeper. "Regularity of custom brings familiarity. A Greek can address a god as his dear god, *philos*. 'Dearest Apollo' cries the master of the house in excitement while looking at the statue which stands in front of his house door." (Burkert, Greek Religion, 274) It is hard to describe the feeling one has for one's patron(s), it truly transcends words. They are a constant presence in your life. And the kharis between you and your patron is personal, even intimate. Anyte wrote: "To Pan the bristly-haired and the Nymphs of the farm-yard, Theodotus the shepherd laid this gift under the crag, because they stayed him when very weary under the parching summer, stretching out to him honey-sweet water in their hands."

*Devotional Acts*

When you have such a love for a god or goddess (whether they be your patron or just close to your heart in other ways), you will want to do special devotions for them. A good place to start is to research them thoroughly, through both primary and secondary sources. Find all the variants of their myths, any festivals or ritual practices we know of, all their attributes and associations. (Pausanias is a good source for a lot of this information; he details some practices and shrines that are otherwise unknown.) Even if you have been worshipping a particular god for years, you will still find new things and gain new insights into that god if you go back and re-read the myths, hymns, and the scholarly writings on him or her.

Build a shrine for them, even a temporary one, and make regular devotions there. Write a hymn, or memorize an ancient hymn to recite frequently. If you are artistic, consider making artwork specifically for and about your god/dess. You might want to make a mix of songs that remind you of that god/dess and play it frequently to put yourself in mind of him or her. Dedicate appropriate activities to the god(s) – for instance, if you are devoted to Poseidon you could learn how to sail, or for Artemis you could take up archery. Do the gods' work in the world – for instance, if you are dedicated to

Hermes, help to care for the homeless or volunteer in a soup kitchen (in ancient Greece food would be left at herms set up at crossroads, which would often be eaten by hungry travelers on their way). Whenever you pass a statue of your god/dess, or anything that reminds you of them, greet it (traditionally by saying "khaire") or blow it a kiss. Make your devotion public – put up a website or post an offering online, or make a contribution to a relevant cause in your god's name (in ancient Greece, major offerings were left at temples with votive inscriptions detailing who left them and why). Hold a theoxenia, a feast in honor of the god, at which the deity is present with you while you eat and drink.

Some gods have traditional devotions particular to them alone. For Hekate, it is customary to leave out a *deipnon*, or dinner, at her statue or a crossroads on the night of the dark moon (the last day of the lunar month). For Hermes, it would be appropriate to scatter some coins at a crossroads or even directly give money to a panhandler – both are echoes of the herm custom I mentioned previously. For Dionysos, a *pannukhia* can be held, an all-night revel. Then of course there are the festivals (ancient and newly created) and smaller devotions based on items special to the gods (burning laurel for Apollon, buying roses for Aphrodite, etc.)

If you are especially dedicated to one or more gods and have been for a long time, you might want to consider some bigger steps. You could begin wearing a piece of jewelry all the time that reminds you of them – such as an owl pendant for Athene. You could devote an entire week, month or even year to them, where you celebrate all their festivals and holy days without fail, do specific rituals every day, and whatever else you can think of to keep your mind and heart with them at all times.

You might decide to take a new name that is related to them in some way – either for use in the Hellenic community, privately, or even for the world at large. For instance, I have all three of these – a maenad name I use privately with Dionysos, a religious name I use in the community that refers to my role as his devotee, and my last name, which I changed legally many years ago and also alludes to him, albeit subtly. If you are absolutely sure of your dedication to your god, you might also consider getting a devotional tattoo; I know of a number of Hellenic polytheists who have done this, including myself (I am actually working towards making my entire body a walking shrine to my gods by getting numerous devotional tattoos). While tattooing was not common in ancient Greece, it was not completely unheard of either. It is a permanent display of your love for the god, and not to be taken lightly.

Some Hellenic pagans who have patrons choose to formally dedicate themselves as a devotee, priest/ess, etc. (usually in a personalized, solitary ritual, although occasionally as part of a larger group). A few take a different (or additional) route, and ritually marry their patron. The ceremony for marrying a god must be created, because we have no ancient rituals in this case, but the concept is not entirely new. On one night of the Athenian festival called the Anthesteria, the queen was ritually married to Dionysos and was said to then privately consummate that marriage (although we don't know how that was done, since it was kept a secret). Marriage to a god/dess should be taken at least as seriously as marriage between mortals, if not more so. It is an expression of lifelong love, devotion, and partnership. It is also one way to formalize an intimate and even sexual union with a god. There are also Hellenic pagans who enjoy this latter type of relationship but do not feel called to a marriage; rather they consider their patron a lover. Not everyone even wishes to relate to their god(s) in this manner, but I believe it is a valid path for some.

## Pilgrimage

A devotional act that will benefit both the gods and yourself is the adventure of a pilgrimage. There are probably some places even within your own country that would make suitable goals for a pilgrimage – such as the replica of the Parthenon in Nashville, or a particularly stunning statue of a Greek god (not uncommon to find in the U.S.), or even Mardi Gras if you're a Dionysian. (There is some debate as to whether these places that were not intentionally created for the gods themselves qualify as holy. I believe that when a person models something and/or names it after a god, it becomes sacred to that god, at least to a degree.) You could also make a pilgrimage to meet and do ritual with a Hellenic group if you don't have one nearby.

But the biggest and most rewarding pilgrimage, in my opinion, is one to Greece. Yes, we are practicing a living religion that can be meaningful anywhere and doesn't rely on ties to Greece anymore. However, Greece is where our religion began, where our gods were first worshipped – where the gods themselves have favorite haunts and long-established relationships. I can say from experience that traveling through Greece is something which will impact you profoundly, in ways you might not expect. There is information on both domestic holy sites and traveling to Greece on the Neokoroi website; the address is listed at the end of this book.

## Everyday Practice

Plutarch said: "No visits delight us more than those to shrines, no occasions are more pleasant than festivals, nothing we do or see is sweeter than our actions and sights before the gods, when we take part in ceremonies or dances, when we are present at sacrifices or initiations." So how can we have those experiences every day, how do we live with the gods in our lives always? One can start along this path by making a personalized system of sacred days and festivals, as I described in the section about my own festival calendar. While keeping within the traditional framework, you can tailor it to your own life, the gods you hold most dear, etc. You might, for instance, celebrate the anniversary of a significant event in your life (especially one in which you think the gods played a part) every year with a religious festival of your own design – it can still have a Hellenic structure without having an ancient origin.

You could pray upon waking and going to sleep, or at some other specified time during the day (not just formal prayers, but extemporaneous, intimate prayers to the gods you are closest with, so that you begin to develop an ongoing conversation, if you will). This is where the aforementioned prayer beads could come in handy. You could make a habit of stopping in front of your shrine(s) every day and just spending a few moments in silence with the gods. You could start libating a little of every drink you have.

You can mark the sacred days of each month; in *Appendix I* the holy days of ancient Athens are listed, and you can change or add to this list, as long as you stay consistent in your own practice. So you might always honor Athene on the third day of the month as in ancient times, and honor Dionysos on the thirteenth because he is often called "the thirteenth Olympian" (this is actually practiced by some Dionysians).

Again, it is acceptable to essentially "make it up" as long as it makes sense and keeps in the general tradition of Hellenismos. While your religious life will inevitably change and evolve to some extent over time, it is also important to try to stick to what you've planned (unless it is no longer working at all), to establish a personal tradition, and to give to the gods everything you have promised.

One of my favorite things to do is to just spend time with the gods casually – not as part of formal ritual, not for festivals, but just "hang out" while in the proper state of mind (what I called "ritual consciousness" earlier), where you are aware of the gods, talk to them, share your space with them, maybe listen to music or read poetry, but mostly just exist in the same time and place with them for an hour or two. I think this is just as important as all the more "official" forms of religious practice, because it brings your interaction with them into your everyday life, where you can start to feel them as a constant presence.

## "Everything is Full of Gods"

We must also endeavor to notice the gods all around us, wherever we are, all the time. In part this can take the form of recognizing the gods' messages for us in omens and the like. But it goes beyond that. Once you start actually feeling the presence of the gods in everything around you, it will change your whole perception of the world, and add a new dimension to your religious practice as well. "With this mindset, the chasm between the sacred and the profane, the divine and the commonplace narrows – and perhaps even disappears altogether. Participation in life becomes a constant holy task when one keeps their mind fixed upon the Gods who permeate the world." (Lewis, *A Temple of Words*, 65)

How do you attain such a state? How do perceive the gods in the world around you? Todd Jackson suggested the following method on the HellenicPagan internet discussion group: "I see it like this: imagine for a moment all the Gods wearing cloaks, those cloaks cover literally everything. No aspect of the world remains untouched. But the God, the Goddess, who wears the cloak, could be anywhere, even very distant. It might be worthwhile to tell someone who cannot see the God, and who wishes to do so – 'Try to perceive the cloak.' This anyone ought to be able to do." This is certainly a good beginning; and you can even take it further.

One practice that I have found to be surprisingly transformative is this: stop, wherever you are, and look around you, and try to identify things that are special to any one of the gods. For instance, that gate over there is sacred to Hermes as god of boundaries; that pigeon on the ground is from the dove family and therefore sacred to Aphrodite; that water fountain is sacred to the nymphs; that statue reminds me of Artemis, that oak tree nearby belongs to Zeus. Do this practice as often as you can, whenever it occurs to you. At first, it is just an intellectual exercise, although still a useful one as it strengthens your knowledge of the gods and their associations. But over time (or perhaps all at once someday, as it happened to me) you will cross over from intellectual understanding to spiritual and emotional understanding: that oak *is* Zeus, that gate *is* Hermes. And then suddenly, as Thales said, "Everything is full of gods." You don't just know it in your head, you feel it in your heart, in your soul. Your perception is forever altered (although you might find it helpful to keep doing the practice to hold onto that insight).

Taking these steps brings Hellenismos from a dry reconstruction of an ancient practice into a full and vibrant living religion, a bridge between yourself and the gods. However, this is not the end of the possibilities; for some people, there is a strong desire to get even closer to the gods, to experience their mysteries directly. For this, we must move on to the next chapter.

# CHAPTER FIVE

# Mysticism, Magic & Mysteries

# MYSTICISM, MAGIC & MYSTERIES

Through the millennia, in cultures all over the world, some people have sought direct contact with their gods. It is rarely the mainstream aspect of any religion, but it is often a part of it in some way. We usually call this mysticism today, but a mystic is not always a hermit living in seclusion, nor a nun lying enraptured in a convent. In ancient Greece, there were various ways one could encounter the gods directly – some fall under the category of mysticism, others might be called magic (a loaded term these days, but unfortunately there is no other adequate word), and there were also the rituals known as the Mysteries. Hellenismos can be practiced without delving into any of these things. However, it is untrue that they do not have any place in our religion at all. It is possible, within the context of traditional Hellenic polytheism, to achieve an intimate communion with deity. "What is characteristic of the Greek religion is not the place relationship of its gods with men but the fact that it could be entirely suspended, so as to make their meeting possible." (Kerenyi, *Religion of the Greeks and Romans*, 189)

## Meeting the Gods

What do we mean when we say "direct contact" with the gods? Well, usually a spiritual context is being referred to – a meeting between our spiritual selves and the deity. Or perhaps even a semi-physical event, where a person has a literal vision of a god. But occasionally this meeting can take a physical form. We read in the myths of the gods walking the earth and interacting with mortals. We assume that either this is a total fabrication, or belongs to a long-ago time and never happens anymore. I think, however, there might be another explanation.

"Olympians adopt all manner of incognitos for their appearances before Homeric heroes, sometimes cloaking themselves in a fog, sometimes assuming the likeness of a mortal familiar to the character whom they visit, sometimes transforming themselves into the birds that descend effortlessly from their lofty perches." (Steiner, 80)

When picturing the stories from mythology in our heads, I think many of us tend to see them with Hollywood-type glamour and special effects. There is Zeus, magically morphing into a shower of gold to rain upon Danae. Or Aphrodite, approaching Anchises as a mortal woman but with her beautiful robe practically glowing, revealing her true self. Or Apollon, leading his priests to Delphi in the form of a dolphin. These things belong to the realm of mythology, not our modern reality. If they ever did happen, they certainly don't happen now.

But what if we take a different view? What if the people who lived those stories experienced them in a much more natural and tangible way than we have imagined – perhaps not as ordinary events, but not supernatural either? What if, what we would see as an amazing but purely physical event – say, coming upon a deer in the woods, who then looks into your eyes for several moments before running away – they would have seen as meeting Artemis in the woods, looking right into her eyes.

Take the previous example of Apollon – instead of the god miraculously changing from an anthropomorphic physical form into that of a dolphin, and then leading the Cretan priests to land, what if a dolphin simply appeared at the side of their boat (as is not uncommon, the same thing happened to a friend of mine in the waters near Delphi), but they knew it to be Apollon and followed it because they were smart enough to follow a god? What if they didn't need to see the recognizable god actually change into the dolphin, to understand (through experience, through faith, through gut instinct) that the dolphin was nonetheless the god himself?

I mentioned that this happened to a friend – she was vacationing in Greece, took a boat ride to the bay near Delphi, and as she approached that sacred place, a dolphin appeared alongside the boat as if it were guiding her there. She certainly noted that this was a special occurrence, and that it might even be a "sign" (from the gods, or the universe, I'm not sure of her precise spiritual beliefs), but she never entertained the notion that it could be something even greater. And I doubt that many of us would – it seems hubristic or even crazy to believe that a god could be present in such a physical, *real* form, especially in order to communicate with us. But I think we might be missing out on something by dismissing the possibility.

"Odysseus, one of the few heroes who succeeds in making his tutelary goddess reveal herself, knows that he stands as exception to the common rule: 'It is difficult for a mortal encountering you to recognize you, goddess,' he remarks to Athena, 'for you are able to liken yourself to everything.'"(Steiner, 80)

I first had this idea many years ago while reading the beginning of Marion Zimmer Bradley's *The Firebrand*. She re-imagines the story of Leda and Zeus – instead of a swan, Zeus comes to Leda in the body of her husband. She sees Tyndareus walking to her as lightning sparks in the sky above, and she knows that she is looking at Zeus, that he has essentially possessed Tyndareus and is using that form to make contact with her. Through that physical incarnation (and yet, not some unbelievable manifestation out of thin air, but simply the temporary possession of an already physical form), he is even able to impregnate her. I believe that this type of experience is how many of the encounters between mortals and gods took place, how they appeared to the people involved, and how they can *still* happen today.

I know that many people believe that the gods send omens and signs, and I do too. I know that sometimes, when a hawk appears at a poignant moment, that hawk is a sign from Hermes, sending me a message. What I am suggesting here is that sometimes, the hawk might be Hermes himself in hawk form, come for some purpose for which a messenger wouldn't suffice. This might even seem like a subtle difference, but I think it is important. Because it opens up the possibility that the gods are indeed speaking to us, even coming to us, actually, immanently, right now. That it is not only mystics who have direct experiences with the gods, but perhaps merely only them who recognize those experiences as such. And also that we might be praying for our gods to appear before us, and then turning a blind eye to them when they do.

So, if all this is true (and that is a matter of faith, and one that each person must decide for themselves), how do we take off the blinders? Well, for one thing, the next time you pray and receive something you see as a "sign," take a closer look. Test the experience (I once had a crow follow me for quite a ways, stopping and starting again when I did, after I asked it to show me if it was more than just a crow). Especially if the thing in question directly approaches you in some way, or is doing something totally out of the ordinary. If you pray to Hermes and encounter a homeless man just afterwards, it may be a sign. If that man tells you something he should not have known, appears to know you, and gives you pertinent advice, he may not be just a man (this happened to another friend of mine).

Of course, sometimes a crow is just a crow. And yes, there is a danger here of losing touch with reality, seeing gods everywhere even when there are none, believing everything is directed at you. There are methods to counteract this – share your experience with a trusted friend and get their objective opinion; confirm or deny it through divination or look for a follow-up omen; consult a seer; review your dreams afterwards; keep a healthy dose of humor and skepticism within you at all times; etc. But I think it is still worth a deeper look, despite the risks. Because just consider the possibility that the gods are right in front of us, and we don't even recognize them! That the kinds of things that happen between gods and mortals in the myths could happen now, to us, if we open ourselves up to the experience!

Ecstatic States

Now on to the topic of spiritual communion with deity. This is usually achieved in what is called an altered state of consciousness, or an ecstatic state (from the Greek word *ekstasis*, outside oneself). While in this altered state, the lines between our world and the world of the gods become blurred. One experiences the presence of the gods more closely than when in a normal frame of mind. With practice, one can even learn to communicate with the gods in this trance state, to receive visions, hear their voices, speak prophecies, etc. One might even be so open that one can be possessed by a god/dess (this can cross gender boundaries as well, i.e., a woman may be possessed by a male god and vice versa), though this can be frightening if the person is not prepared.

Ecstatic states can be entered into with many different techniques. We do not know much about the ancient ways in this matter – one of the most well-known example of ekstasis in ancient Greece, the cult of the maenads, is shrouded in myth and specific only to one god, although we can take some ideas from their practices – but we can also draw on the knowledge of other cultures around the world. Techniques include rhythmic chanting and drumming, wild dance, fasting, sensory deprivation, intense prayer and focus, controlled infliction of pain (not recommended unless you know what you are doing) and intoxication or ingestion of psychoactive drugs.

A note about the latter – certain plants have been used for millennia to achieve altered states of consciousness for spiritual purposes. They were always consumed in the proper context, with respect for the plant and its effects; they were not abused and rarely used recreationally. Today many of these plants, commonly called entheogens ("that which generates god within") are illegal in the U.S. and other countries. Some however are still legal and available: amanita muscaria (fly agaric) mushroom, salvia divinorum (not legal in all states), blue lotus, syrian rue, and more (even alcohol can be considered an entheogen if used in that context). If you decide to utilize any of these tools in your ecstatic work, be careful; learn the proper dosages and possible side effects. Pay respect to the plant and do not use it lightly. These are sacred gifts from the gods, which we can use to get closer to them; they are not toys.

Learning how to achieve altered states of consciousness is a process and will probably not happen on your first try. Even when you are experienced in these matters, you will find that there are always new levels to be explored. If you want to begin learning this art, I suggest you start with small rituals with a particular god/dess as a focus. Choose a day where you will have time and space to yourself. Fast for at least half a day beforehand to cleanse your system and focus your mind. Purify yourself with khernips. Then find a good spot, preferably near your shrine if you have one.

It is good to begin with a formal ritual, prayer and offering, both to get you "in the mood" and to ask the god/dess for their help. You may want to light candles, darken the room, and even put a veil over your face to further distort your perception of the outside world (although you can also choose to keep your eyes closed). It might also be helpful at first to play some kind of background music especially if you live in a place with lots of outside noise (appropriate music can be fast or slow, but should be instrumental if possible since words will likely distract you). I find it powerful to burn a lot of incense, herbs or other plants associated with the god or that remind me of his or her presence; for instance, when doing prophetic trance for Apollon, I fill the room with the smoke of burning bay (laurel) leaves. Not only is this psychologically effective, but the overwhelming sensation of the heavy, clouded air I'm breathing enhances the experience physiologically. Of course, you have to be careful not to smoke yourself out of the room, or set off the fire alarm, which would certainly ruin the mood.

Then you can go from there, with whatever methods seem most natural to you – chanting the god's epithets, for instance, or dancing in front of a fire. I found in my experience that at first it was helpful to have at least a little taste of intoxicants (even just a glass of wine would do) to get me into a slightly "fuzzy" state, from which it was easier to slip into ekstasis. After more experience, that was no longer always necessary. You will find your own way - experiment, but remember to be careful.

How do you know when you've made that contact with the gods? Georg Misch (*A History of Autobiography in Antiquity*, 1951) quotes Aristides as saying: "It was a sort of sense of contact and a clear realization that the god himself had come; an intermediate state between sleeping and waking, a desire to look and at the same time a fear that he would go away first; a listening and hearing half in dream, half awake; the hair on end and tears of joy and an inward swelling with delight - what human beings could find words to describe it? Those who are of the initiated will understand a recognize it."

Once you are in the proper state of mind, there are a few options. You can simply enjoy the feeling of closeness with the god(s). You can let it inspire you to make art or music or write a hymn, if you are so inclined. You can perform divination. Or you can attempt more direct communication with the gods, through a process sometimes called prophetic trance, which can include having visions, hearing their voices, receiving insights, etc. (more on that below).

It is hard to describe how it feels to really be in an ecstatic state. All I can say is that you will know when you are there - and that as you progress, you will keep finding deeper states that make the first times seem pale by comparison. If you do this long enough and often enough, it may start to bleed into your "normal" life - you may find yourself feeling altered during your everyday activities. This might be disconcerting, but it is in fact what many mystics aspire to. Being able to exist in the gods' direct presence at any time is truly living with the gods - a step beyond the types of exercises I mentioned at the end of the last chapter.

You might also feel called to set aside certain periods of time in which you completely devote yourself to some kind of ascetic practice, in order to break down your own internal barriers and therefore be closer to the gods. Examples of such include extended fasting, periods of complete silence, celibacy, and personal sacrifices (akin to the kind made by devout Christians for Lent). These are difficult but rewarding hardships. They show you, and the gods, what you're really made of, and what you're willing to endure to get closer to them.

## Prophetic Trance

Seers were an important part of ancient Greek religion. "The vast majority of Greeks believed that the gods desired to communicate with mortals, that they did so through signs of various kinds, and that there were religious experts who could correctly interpret those signs." (Flower, 8) While some seers specialized in interpreting omens and signs, others revealed the gods' messages through direct inspiration. Not all seers were universally accepted, but some were extremely respected.

In modern Hellenismos, this is a tricky issue. Some people wish for a return of such seers in our religion (after all, we still have questions for the gods, need help or guidance, and most people have trouble contacting the gods directly at will), but many are cautious or downright skeptical of such an ability even existing, much less in the person of some modern worshipper of the gods. Some question the ability of anyone to have such power.

Having actually been doing divination for a long time myself, and prophetic trance for the past several years, I'm coming to see it much less as an issue of the person having power. It is more like a combination of natural talent and hard work. Learning how to achieve that kind of openness, to let enough of yourself fall away to actually be able to receive communication directly from a deity, is extremely hard. I think it's a rare case that someone has really strong abilities in that area without having to work at it. Now, it's certainly easier if you have a basic knack for it to begin with (maybe impossible without that?) but it's still work.

The metaphor I often use is of an artist – you may have natural drawing ability, but you will still have to train for many years before you become an artist of any caliber. But you wouldn't think of an accomplished artist as claiming to have any special powers. So if the gods do indeed exist, and have the power to communicate with us, what's so crazy about a person training themselves to be, essentially, a good listener? To me, that's no more "powerful" than being able to track an animal in the woods, or bench press 300 pounds. They all take patience, hard work, and some natural ability to begin with, but might seem almost magical to a person who could never dream of doing those things.

If you feel called to the work of prophetic trance, there is not much I can convey in words (at least, not within the scope of this book) to help you begin, other than to recommend that you do a lot of reading on cross-cultural means of attaining trance (since little exists from ancient Greece), and mostly practice getting into (and maintaining) altered states of consciousness. Also, it is important to build strong relationships with the gods, especially with a god related to prophecy (the obvious choice being Apollon). Knowledge of mechanical forms of divination is helpful, but for this work it is necessary to put the cards down, and open the mind directly to the voice of the gods.

To begin this process, empty your mind, the way I suggested in my section on divination and listening to the gods. Ask the god(s) to guide you, or ask a specific question. Let whatever images or words form in your mind come, but don't cling to them. It's kind of like a focused train of thought, but in this case the thoughts should ideally be coming from outside yourself. Eventually, with the right combination of openness and focus, these images and/or words will coalesce into something meaningful. With some experience, it will be clear to you when you're getting a true response, instead of your own mental debris.

It is a long and difficult process if done correctly, but I hope more people are willing to take it up, so that we might have a collection of seers in the future who can be conduits between mortal questions and the divine answers.

Ancient Mystics

There are plenty of examples from ancient Greece of people who had intimate relationships with deities, who achieved ecstatic states and otherwise delved into mysticism. As I mentioned before, a familiar example is the cult of the maenads, the frenzied female devotees of Dionysos. There is some confusion between the maenads portrayed in myth and the "real", historical maenads. Some believe therefore that the miraculous and sometimes supernatural acts attributed to the maenads – tearing apart a live bull and eating it raw, for instance – are all the stuff of myth, and that the historical maenads performed fairly standard rituals for their god. I think, however, that the stories may well have represented actual practices, and that the line between mythical and historical maenadism is blurry at best.

The maenads were said to have supernatural strength, and be impervious to weapons and fire. They charmed snakes and wore them in their hair. These accounts might seem unbelievable until one begins finding similar examples of such phenomena from cultures world-wide, including more well-documented events in recent times. Rituals are often performed in India, for instance, where worshippers pierce themselves with large spikes and walk on fire, all without showing any pain. They do this partly by inducing an altered state of consciousness through dance, music, and worship of their gods. I believe this is exactly what was happening for the maenads (or at least some of them). Through frenzied dance, intoxication by wine, and love of Dionysos, they achieved a state of direct contact with the god, who could then enable them to do almost anything.

An example of a different type of altered state (that of prophetic trance, as discussed above) is that of the Pythia. An older woman who lived in the temple complex of Apollon at Delphi, the Pythia was called upon to deliver oracles from the god's mouth. Her methods for achieving contact with the god are not known. Old stories attribute the ability to the fumes rising up from a crack in the earth's surface beneath the Pythia's seat – while possible evidence for these gases has recently been discovered (I recommend *The Oracle* by William J. Broad for a current and fascinating discussion of this topic), it still seems unlikely that they were the sole reason behind the Pythia's trance state. Some say she inhaled the burning laurel leaves – while laurel is not hallucinogenic, the connection it has with Apollon might have helped fuel her trance psychologically. Perhaps she was just adept at entering an ecstatic state on her own, through her devotion to Apollon.

Whatever the case, she was able to speak his words to those who sought his advice or prophecy. It is certainly possible that, as some have asserted, the priests in the temple changed what she said or even fabricated it entirely at times. But I do believe that at least some of the time, the Pythia was able to achieve a trance state and contact Apollon directly; and I believe it can still be done today, as I discussed above.

Another example of a close relationship between a human and a deity is that of the nympholepts. Some of these men lived in caves sacred to the nymphs and tended them as shrines, which other people could visit. These nympholepts sometimes spent their whole lives in service to the nymph or nymphs of that specific area, and their inscriptions show that they loved them dearly, even intimately. "Onesagoras, another nympholept who filled a cave in third-century Cyprus with dedications to an individual nymph, referred to her as sister, daughter, and possibly as lover." (Larson, 16) The nympholepts also often possessed the gift of prophecy, a gift that was believed to be given by the nymphs – and a type of ecstatic state as well. Nympholepts were marginalized by society to an extent (some of which was self-imposed), like many mystics, but they were still a part of it.

Other marginalized figures in ancient Greece are sometimes called the Greek "shamans." They were said to be able to detach and transport their souls (a practice known in modern paganism as "astral travel"), speak prophecies, remember their reincarnations, bilocate, heal sickness, and even suspend their lifespans (enabling them to appear almost immortal). A famous example is Aristeas, a man who traveled to the fabled land of the Hyperboreans, could take the shape of a raven, and spread the cult of his god everywhere he went. Another is Epimenides, who slept for 57 years in a cave, and who subsisted entirely on magical food given to him by the nymphs. It is probable that many tales of these men were exaggerated, but I think it is also possible that some of the stories are true, and they did indeed master certain "supernatural" abilities due to their spiritual focus and power – skills similar to those of the sadhus of India.

## Acts of Magic

Magic has occupied a sometimes controversial place in modern Hellenismos, as some people still insist that it doesn't belong within the religion proper, or that it is simply a mimicry of Wicca or other neo-paganisms. This bias against magic in Greek polytheism is present in the scholarly communities as well.

"In the past, scholars have denigrated magical activities as the domain of the superstitious, and therefore not worth the attention of serious students of religion....It is true that philosophers developed rarefied notions of religion, but they were not at all typical. The universal and commonplace acceptance of magic, among all classes, is easily proved from the evidence. In such a world it is on general grounds not likely that magic was compartmentalized, and its mentality abandoned when the people partook in rituals more readily recognized as 'religious' by the modern scholar. The phenomenon of magic, in fact, cannot be separated from any serious understanding of ancient religion. That it tends to be separated in the minds of students is the results of the historical development of the discipline rather than any inherent necessity." (Robert L. Fowler, "Greek Magic, Greek Religion," in *Oxford Readings in Greek Religion* ed. Buxton)

Today everyone has a different idea of what constitutes "magic" – it's certainly not an essential part of Greek paganism, ancient or modern, and the religion can be practiced devoutly and properly without it, on a personal level. But if you are attracted to magic in some way, you might wish to learn more from some of the books I have listed in the bibliography.

Aside from the special individuals I mentioned above, there were some types of "magic" that anyone could perform, in the right circumstances. Divination, discussed earlier, can fall into this category, as can healing through dream incubation. There are other types of folk healing as well, involving certain herbs or talismans.

One of the most complicated forms of magic is necromancy. This does not mean bringing the dead back to life literally, but rather raising the spirit of a dead person in order to get information or make it do something for you. In some ways, the rites of necromancy were similar to other Greek rituals – a purification, libations, animal sacrifice, prayer, etc. But there were differences too – the rite took place between sunset and dawn, the offerings were made in a pit with a fire burning in it, and the prayers were addressed to the khthonioi and the ghosts of the dead themselves. Sometimes threats and curses were used as well, including *kolossoi*, human-shaped dolls that were abused in various ways in order to enact some hold over the person they represented. Often a blood offering of some kind was made, as that was thought to "feed" the dead and make it possible to interact with them – like when Odysseus pours blood out for the spirits in the *Odyssey*, and those who drink it regain their memory and awareness for a brief time. While necromancy is often considered "evil," it can be done respectfully (minus the curses and such) and is not inherently wrong. Making offerings to the dead spirits in exchange for their help isn't really any different from other forms of kharis.

## Mystery Cults

The final topic that needs to be discussed here is the Mysteries. There were a few major Mystery cults in ancient Greece – the most famous are the Eleusinian Mysteries (dedicated to Demeter and Persephone), but there were also similar rites for Dionysos, the Kabeiroi, and others that we know little about. Although many thousands of people attended the Mystery rites, they were kept strictly secret, and as such we do not have many details about them, but we do know that the purported goal of being initiated into most of them was to achieve a favored afterlife. Hades was believed to be a dismal place, and the souls of the dead mere shades of their past selves, with no memory or consciousness – to bypass that existence and instead enter the blessed Elysian Fields, to keep one's memory and enjoy one's afterlife, these were surely powerful promises.

We do know that the Eleusinian Mysteries culminated in some kind of epiphany, perhaps of Persephone herself. Whatever it was, it was considered both *aporrheton* (forbidden to speak of to the uninitiated) and *arrheton* (beyond words, unable to be expressed at all). A lot of attention is paid to what precisely was revealed during those rites – an image of the goddess, an ear of corn, there are many theories. I think, however, that these speculations are missing the point.

I believe that the Mystery rites were carefully engineered by experienced priests and priestesses to give people an ecstatic experience, to put the initiates into an altered state of consciousness in which they could encounter the goddess on their own. Aristotle, when referring to the Mysteries, said: "The candidate did not have to learn, but to experience something, and to come to be in a certain state of mind."

Taking that a step further, I think that the reason the Mysteries were supposed to ensure a blessed afterlife for the initiate was that they broached the veil between the worlds, they gave the person a direct experience of the gods, something that would stay with them even after death, and would give them the ability to retain their consciousness and not slip into the shadows of Hades with everyone else. If you strengthen your spirit, and experience a real closeness to and familiarity with the gods, perhaps you can keep your awareness, your *self*, intact through the process of dying, and reach the other side whole.

So when we speak of reviving the Mysteries (as some do), I think the focus should not be on reconstructing whatever details we do know, but on crafting a similar experience, an initiation that brings the person before the gods themselves. It is an intimidating task, to be sure, but one which could potentially benefit us all.

# AFTERWORD

It is often asked, did the gods allow the ancient worship to die out? I cannot answer this question, but I do believe that either way, they are behind the current revival. So many people are being called to this path, it seems that every day there is a new member. And we are such a passionate group, so filled with love for the gods, a desire to do right by them (although how this should be accomplished is frequently debated), and a wish to see our religion evolve and thrive. I hope with this book to do my small part to encourage the progress of Hellenic polytheism.

To every person who has felt the call of the gods of ancient Hellas, who pours a libation or recites a hymn, who strives to be ever closer to them – you are not alone. Even separated by many miles, we are all here, worshipping the same gods, in our own ways. With us, the tradition of Hellenismos continues to live, even in this modern world. We stand at an exciting point in history: the rebirth of the ancient pagan religions only a few decades old, all of us working to build strong and meaningful pagan faiths today. I look forward to what the future holds for us all.

# APPENDIX I.
## The Ancient Athenian Calendar and Major Festivals

The ancient Greek year began on the new moon after the summer solstice. The beginning of each month was fixed by the observation of the lunar crescent after the dark moon (called the "new moon"). It is believed that each "day" began at sunset, lasting until the next sunset (although there is evidence that this was not the case in every area). Due to the irregularities of a twelve-month lunar calendar, the month of Poseideon was occasionally repeated when necessary to maintain the integrity of the calendar year.

Certain days of every month were devoted to particular deities. They are as follows –

**First day**: Noumenia – the new moon festival
**Second**: Agathos Daimon
**Third**: Athene and the Graces
**Fourth**: Aphrodite, Hermes, Herakles and Eros
**Sixth**: Artemis
**Seventh**: Apollon
**Eighth**: Poseidon
**Last three days**: all chthonic deities
**Last day** (dark moon): Hekate

Here follows a list of the months in order (beginning with the new year). Each month is named, with an explanation of the origin of the name in parentheses. Then the major festivals are listed by the day they begin, with a short description of ritual and/or purpose.

Remember that this is only the festival calendar of Athens. Many demoi had different names for the months and celebrated different festivals.

HEKATOMBAION (an epithet of Apollon, alluding to his role as accepter of sacrifices)

4: **Aphrodisia** - The bathing festival of Aphrodite and Peitho (Persuasion). The temple was purified with dove's blood, then the altars were anointed and the two statues were carried in a procession to the washing place.

12: **Kronia** - A festival in honor of Kronos as god of the harvest, portrayed with a reaping scythe. A huge harvest feast was held, where slaves were invited to dine with their masters.
28: **Panathenaia** - The celebration of Athene's birthday. A vigil was held the night before the Panathenaic procession. At sunrise a sacrifice was made to Eros and Athene at the altar of Eros in the Academy, then a torch race brought the sacred fire to the altar of Athene. Every fourth year, the Greater Panathenaia was held, when a new robe was given to the goddess. A huge procession brought the robe to her statue in her temple, where it was placed on Athene's knees, and later stored in the treasury; she was officially re-robed during the Plunteria. Sacrifices were also made to Athene Hugieia (Health) and Nike. The three or four days following the procession featured contests of sport and art.

METAGEITNION (an epithet of Apollon, "changing neighbors")

Unspecified: **Metageitnios** - Named after Apollon's epithet, it may have been a festival of the neighborhood.
Unspecified: **Herakles' Day** - A celebration of Herakles by athletes in the gymnasium in Kunosarges.

BOIDROMION (an epithet of Apollon, meaning to help in response to a shout)

5: **Genesia** - The Athenian state festival in honor of the dead, especially those who died in wars.
6: **Kharisteria** - The feast of Artemis Agrotera (the huntress). After the victory at Marathon, this became a commemoration of that battle, and was known as Kharisteria, "Thanksgiving."
7: **Boidromia** - A festival of thanksgiving for Apollon as a god who rescued people in war.
15-21: **Eleusinian Mysteries** - The mystery rites of Demeter and Persephone, held at Eleusis.

PUANEPSION ("boiled beans," a ritual food)

5: **Proerosia** - An agricultural festival of Demeter held at Eleusis, the name means "preliminary to ploughing." Offerings of first fruits (mostly grain) were given to Demeter to ask for her blessing at the beginning of the sowing season.

7: **Puanepsia** - Apollon was offered a sacrifice of a he-goat and a lamb, and a meal was held for the god. During the procession, each boy carried an eiresione, the traditional sign of a suppliant. However, on this day, the eiresione (normally a bough of olive wreathed with wool) was made of laurel, and was decorated with pastries shaped like wines, harps and cups, along with real fruit. The boys carried the boughs from house to house, begging for food, and singing. If the occupant gave them something, they would give him an eiresione to bless his house. The ritual food that gave its name to this festival and this month consisted of a mixture of boiled legumes. According to myth, Theseus and his crew returned to Athens on this day, and offered Apollon this dish, made from the remains of their provisions.

7: **Oskhophoria** - The celebration of the vine harvest, when men carried vine branches with the grapes still clinging to them through the town in a procession. Hymns about the harvest and wine-making were sung. A ritual meal was held, where legends were told and acted out.

8: **Theseia** - A festival honoring Theseus, the son of Poseidon. There was a procession, sacrifices, athletic contests, and a feast of meat and a porridge of wheat and milk.

9: **Stenia** - A nocturnal women's festival for Demeter and Persephone in preparation for the Thesmophoria. The women insulted each other light-heartedly to commemorate the way Iambe made the grieving Demeter laugh. Fertility objects were thrown into pits in the sanctuary of Demeter, including bread in the shape of snakes and phalluses, and sacrificed pigs.

11-13: **Thesmophoria** - An all-female agricultural festival in honor of Demeter and Persephone, held in Demeter's hillside sanctuary. On the first day, the women climbed the hill and made camp, sleeping on the ground in huts. On the second day, the women sat on the ground and fasted from all solid food (except pomegranate seeds) in sympathy for Demeter's mourning. They taunted each other in iambic verse, in imitation of Iambe and Demeter. On the third day, there was a torch-light ceremony, because Demeter sought Persephone by torch-light. This may have been when the objects were removed from the earth by purified priestesses, and placed on the altars of the goddesses. Later this "compost" was mixed with the grain to be sown the following month. Then the rest of the day was spent in joyous celebration.

30: **Khalkeia** - A festival of smiths, associated with Hephaistos and Athene. It was a day of rest from work, and a procession of workers moved through the town carrying baskets of corn. Later, a feast was held.

MAIMAKTERION ("blustering," epithet of Zeus)

Unspecified: **Maimakteria** - This month begins the winter season, so people prayed to Zeus Maimaktes (Blustering) to be gentle.
Last third of month: **Pompaia** - A procession dedicated to Zeus Meilikhios (Kindly), a chthonic aspect of Zeus who appears as a snake. A sheep was sacrificed, and its fleece considered magical. A person could purify himself by standing on the wool with his left foot. The fleece, along with a kadukeos, was carried in the procession.

POSEIDEON (Poseidon)

8: **Poseidea** - There was probably a festival in honor of Poseidon during this month, most likely on the eighth day, since that day was sacred to him, but nothing more is known.
Last half of month: **Rural Dionysia** - A simpler and rustic version of the City Dionysia. It included a procession with men carrying a phallus, cake-bearers, revelers and singing. The image of the god was carried into the city to represent Dionysos' arrival. A bull may have been sacrificed, and there were many localized rites, different in every region.
26: **Haloa** - A festival in honor of Demeter and Dionysos, named after the *halos*, or threshing floor. There was a feast including phallus- and pudenda-shaped cakes, but without the foods forbidden in the Eleusinian Mysteries. Women danced around a giant phallus, leaving it offerings. Later in the night, men were admitted, and there was a great revel or orgy for the rest of the night.

GAMELION (month of marriage)

12-15: **Lenaia** - The name of this Dionysian festival may have come from the word for wine-press, or from another name for the maenads. It was celebrated to arouse the slumbering vegetation and bring springtime. There was a representation of Dionysos, probably a wooden pillar, for it was Dionysos Orthos ("the erect") who invented mixing wine and water. There were also dramatic contests, like in so many other Dionysian festivals.

**26: Gamelia** - The anniversary of the sacred marriage of Zeus and Hera, this festival gave its name to the month of marriage. This is a time of spring and new beginnings.

## ANTHESTERION (flowers)

**11-13: Anthesteria** – The Festival of Flowers, as well as a feast of the dead, and a drinking festival centered around Dionysos Limnaios ("of the marshes"). The first day, Pithoigia, was the Opening of the Jars, and the broaching of new wine. Celebrants gathered near the temple and opened wine-jars, pouring libations to Dionysos and drinking the rest. The second day, Khoes, was the Day of Cups. There were drinking matches (where the prize was a skin of wine), and an erotic atmosphere. The next evening, when it was almost the beginning of the next ritual "day," a sacred marriage between the queen and the god was performed in the inner chamber of the temple (which was only open for that night). The last day, Khutroi, was the Day of Pots, devoted to the cult of the dead. Pots containing cooked vegetables and seeds (traditional food for the dead) were left out for the wandering spirits. However, precautions were taken to prevent the spirits from coming too close: people chewed hawthorn, smeared their doors with pitch, and tied ropes around the temples. At the end of the festival, they drove out the spirits, saying, "Out you Keres, it is no longer Anthesteria!"

**23 or 28: Diasia** - The festival of Zeus Meilikhios (Kindly), the chthonic Zeus who appears as a snake. Offerings were made of cakes shaped like animals, grains, and other fertility foods. The whole offering was burnt.

**Unspecified: Lesser Eleusinian Mysteries** - These were the preparations for the next year's Mysteries, held at Agrai on the banks of the Illissos.

## ELAPHEBOLION (an epithet of Artemis, "shooter of deer")

**6: Elaphebolia** - Festival of Artemis, where she was offered cakes shaped like stags, made from dough, honey and sesame-seeds.

**8 or 9: Asklepieia** - Festival of Asklepios, including a large sacrifice and common meal with the god.

**9-13: Greater (or City) Dionysia** - The largest of the Dionysian festivals, held in Athens, where Dionysos had a theatre and where dithyrambs and plays were performed. Before the festival began, a statue representing the god was placed on the road to the city, offered a sacrifice, and escorted back to the temple, thereby bringing in the god to the festival. On the first day, there was a procession with various offerings, which led into the komos, or revel, a nightlong feast and celebration. The next few days were set aside for the famous dramatic contests of Athens.

14 or 17: **Pandia** - A festival of Zeus.

MOUNIKHION (festival of Artemis)

4: **Feast of Eros** - This may have been held on the fourth due to the god's connection with Aphrodite; no more is known.

6 or 16: **Mounikhia** - Festival of Artemis as the moon goddess and mistress of the animals. A procession of girls carrying boughs came to the shrine of Apollon and Artemis. A she-goat was sacrificed to the goddess, along with other offerings. Another procession consisted of people carrying *amphiphontes* (shining-all-around), round cakes containing lit candles arranged in a circle.

19: **Olympieia** - Festival of Olympian Zeus, including a huge sacrifice, possibly of a bull.

THARGELION (festival of Apollon)

6-7: **Thargelia** - This festival marked the birthdays of Apollon and Artemis. The first day was devoted to purification. Two poor people were chosen as *pharmakoi* (scapegoats), each representing the women or the men; they were fed well, then beaten in order to purify the city. The second day was devoted to offerings of first fruits, called the *thargelos* (a vegetable and grain stew or possibly bread). Hymn-singing contests were held for the men's and boy's choirs.

Last Week (25?): **Plunteria** - This festival was dedicated to washing the ancient statue of Athene Polias (Guardian of the City). The temple had been cleaned, and Athene's eternal flame relit, by her priestesses a few days before. Women removed the robe and jewelry from the statue, which was then wrapped and carried in a procession to the washing place. Figs were offered to the goddess on the shore. After washing, the statue was taken by torchlight procession back to the temple and clothed with a new, clean robe (from the Panathenaia) and adorned with jewelry. This day was considered inauspicious because Athene was absent from the city.

## SKIROPHORION (festival of Demeter)

**Beginning (3?):** **Arrhephoria** - A hidden rite revolving around two young priestesses of Athene, called the Arrhephoroi ("Carriers of Unspoken Things"). After living in Athene's temple for two years, they performed various secret rituals, including carrying a package by a secret path to the sanctuary of Aphrodite in the Gardens, and bringing back another secret package. Then they were replaced by two new girls.

**12: Skiraphoria** - Also called the Skira, the festival of the cutting and threshing of the grain. Priests and priestesses went in procession to the Skiron, the sacred sanctuary of Demeter and Kore, where the first sowing took place. The festival was celebrated mostly by women, who abstained from sex on this day in order to bring fertility to the land. They threw cakes shaped like snakes and phalluses as well as pigs into the sacred caverns of Demeter. The men had a race carrying vine-branches from the sanctuary of Dionysos to the temple of Athene Skiras. The winner was given the Fivefold Cup, which contained wine, honey, cheese, corn and olive oil. He shared this drink with the goddess, pouring her a libation to request her blessing on the fruits of the season.

**14: Dipolieia** - This was a festival of Zeus as god of the city. Barley and wheat were placed on an altar. When the sacrificial bull ate the grain, he was killed by a priest, who immediately threw down his axe and fled. The axe was later tried formally for murder. (This festival was considered antiquated by the fourth century.)

**Last Day: Sacrifice to Zeus the Savior and Athene the Savior** - A sacrifice (possibly a bull) was made on the last day of the old year to ensure good health and well-being for the coming year.

# APPENDIX II.

# Plants, Animals, Places, & Activities Sacred to Specific Gods and Goddesses

**Animals**
bear – Artemis
bees – Nymphs
boar – Ares
bull – Poseidon, Dionysos, Zeus, River Gods
cock – Hermes
cow – Hera
crane – Hephaistos
cuckoo – Hera
deer – Artemis
dog – Artemis, Hekate
dolphin – Apollon, Poseidon
donkey – Hephaistos
dove – Aphrodite
eagle – Zeus
fish – Poseidon
fox – Dionysos
goat – Dionysos, Pan
hawk – Hermes
horse – Poseidon, Haides, The Anemoi
lion – Kybele
mouse – Apollon
owl – Athene
panther – Dionysos
peacock – Hera
pig – Demeter, Persephone
rabbit – Aphrodite, Eros
ram – Hermes
raven – Apollon
snake – Hermes, Zeus, Dionysos, Apollon, Asklepios,
       Agathos Daimon
swan – Apollon
turtle – Hermes

vulture – Ares
weasel – Hekate
wolf – Zeus, Apollon

**Plants**
anemone – Adonis
apple – Aphrodite
ash tree – Meliads
barley – Demeter
corn – Demeter
crocus – Hermes
fennel – Dionysos, Hephaistos
fig – Dionysos
grapevine – Dionysos
ivy – Dionysos
laurel (bay) – Apollon
mint – Haides
myrtle – Aphrodite, Haides, Persephone
narcissus – Persephone
oak tree – Zeus, Dryads
olive tree – Athene
palm tree – Artemis
pine tree – Dionysos
pomegranate – Persephone, Hera
poplar tree – Persephone, Haides
poppy – Demeter
rose – Aphrodite
rosemary – Haides
wheat – Demeter
willow tree – Hera, Persephone

**Places**
battlefield – Ares, Athene
boundaries – Hermes
caves – Nymphs, Pan
city – Zeus, Athene
crossroads – Hermes, Hekate
fens – Heliads
home – Hestia, Agathos Daimon
hospital – Asklepios, Apollon
marketplace – Hermes
meadows – Leimoniades

mountains – Oreads
ocean – Poseidon, Aphrodite, Nereids
rivers – Potamiads, River Gods
springs –Naiads
streets – Apollon
theatre – Dionysos
woods – Artemis, Pan

**Vocations / Types of People**
archer – Apollon
actor – Dionysos
blacksmith – Hephaistos
father – Zeus
fisherman – Poseidon
healer, doctor – Asklepios, Apollon
homemaker – Hestia
hunter – Artemis, Dionysos (Zagreus)
king – Zeus
lovers – Aphrodite
magician – Hermes, Hekate
merchant – Hermes
messenger – Hermes, Iris
mother – Demeter
poet, musician – Apollon, The Muses
potter – Athene
prophet – Apollon
prostitute – Aphrodite
queen – Hera
sailor – Poseidon
shepherd – Pan, Hermes
smith – Hephaistos
stranger – Zeus
thief – Hermes
transgendered – Dionysos, Hermaphrodite
traveler – Hermes
veterinarian - Artemis
warrior, soldier – Ares, Athene
weaver – Athene

**Misc. Things, Activities, Concepts & Events**
amber – Apollon
art, music, poetry – The Muses, Apollon

battle – Athene, Ares
bow & arrows – Apollon, Artemis, Eros
chariot – Ares
childbirth – Artemis, Eileithuia
crops – Demeter
dawn – Eos
death – Thanatos, Haides
divination – Hermes, Apollon
drama – Dionysos
dreams – Morpheus
drums – Kybele
earthquakes – Poseidon
ecstasy – Dionysos
fate – The Moirai, Tukhe
fire – Hestia, Hephaistos
forge & anvil – Hephaistos
health – Apollon, Asklepios, Hugeia
hearth – Hestia
hunting – Artemis, Pan
justice – Zeus, Dike, Themis
kadukeus – Hermes
keys – Hekate
laughter – Aphrodite
love – Aphrodite
luck – Hermes
lyre – Apollon
magic – Hekate, Hermes
marriage – Hera
martial arts – Ares
mask – Dionysos
medicine – Asklepios
memory – Mnemosune
moon – Selene, Artemis, Hekate
night – Nux, Hekate
oaths – Zeus
panic – Pan
panpipes – Pan
perfume – Aphrodite
phallos – Priapos, Dionysos, Pan, Hermes
prophecy – Apollon
rainbow – Iris
seashells – Aphrodite, Poseidon

seasons – The Horai
sex – Aphrodite, Eros
sceptre – Hera
sickness – Apollon, Asklepios
sky, clouds – Zeus
sleep - Hupnos
spring – Persephone
spear – Ares, Athene
stones – Hermes
strength – Herakles
sun – Helios, Apollon
thunder & lightning – Zeus
torches – Demeter, Hekate, Artemis
tripod – Apollon
victory – Nike
volcano – Hephaistos
war – Ares
wealth – Ploutos
winds – The Anemoi
wine – Dionysos

# APPENDIX III.
# Useful Greek Words and Phrases for Religious Practice

## *Glossary of words*

**aduton**: the "holy of holies," the innermost room of a temple, reserved for special priests, and often where mysteries are revealed

**amphiphontes**: "shining all around" cakes, decorated with a circle of candles, offered to Artemis

**agon** (pl. agones): contest, competition, an important element of most festivals

**aporrheton**: something that it is forbidden to speak of, a religious secret

**arrheton**: something that it is impossible to speak of, a religious experience or wisdom that is beyond words, inexpressible

**astragaloi**: knucklebones, usually from a sheep, used in divination and games

**bomos** (pl. bomoi): an altar on which sacrifices are made, usually a large stone slab or pile of stones

**bothros** (pl. bothroi): a pit that functions as the "altar" for chthonic deities

**daimon** (pl. daimones): a spirit

**deipnon** (pl. deipna) : a banquet, dinner, often used to describe offerings to Hekate on the dark moon

**demos**: an area of land, and/or the people of that land, used by some in Hellenismos to denote a religious group that gathers to worship together

**eiresione**: an olive branch decorated with woolen fillets, used as a mark of supplication and in certain festivals

**ekstasis**: "outside oneself," ecstasy, frenzy, rapture

**enthusiasmos**: "a god is within," possession by a deity

**eranos**: a type of modern ritual group, from the word for a communal meal, a club, a favor

**eukhe**: a prayer

**euphemia**: sacred silence, no ill-omened speech

**eusebeia**: piety, right action

**exegetai**: interpreters of religious law
**hagnos**: holy, pure
**heortai**: seasonal festivals
**hermaion**: a lucky windfall, a gift of Hermes
**herme** (pl. hermai): boundary marker, herm, a pillar of stone with a carved head of Hermes, and usually a phallos as well
**heros**: a hero
**hestia**: the hearth and the fire it contains
**hieros**: holy, sacred
**hiereus**: a priest, sacrificer
**hubris**: pride, arrogance, putting oneself above the gods
**kharisterion**: a thanks offering
**khernips**: pure water in which hands are washed before ritual
**khoe** (pl. khoai): a libation made to the khthonioi
**khresmologos**: an "oracle-monger," someone who keeps records of famous oracles
**khthonioi**: underworld (chthonic) deities and spirits
**kledon** (pl. kledones): an overheard piece of conversation, taken as an omen
**komos**: revel, usually a nocturnal celebration
**mantis** (pl. manteis): prophet, one who speaks the gods' will
**miasma**: pollution
**mustes**: an initiate into the Mysteries
**naos**: temple
**nomos**: custom, tradition
**noumenia**: the "new moon," the first lunar crescent observable after the dark moon, the beginning of the ancient month
**numphai**: the nymphs, literally "brides"
**pannukhia**: a revel or festival that lasts all night long
**panspermia**: "all-grain," a mixture of grains and/or vegetables, a common offerings especially in agricultural festivals
**pharmakoi**: scapegoats, which are believed to carry the miasma of a town away with them when they are beaten or expelled from the community.
**polis**: town, city
**pompe**: procession, the beginning of each festival
**psukhopompos**: a god or spirit who leads the spirits of the dead to the afterlife, psychopomp
**sponde** (pl. spondai): a libation that is sipped by the worshipper and then poured out for the god(s)
**stephanos**: a wreath of flowers and/or leaves worn for ritual occasions

**symposia**: dinner parties at which men met to eat, drink wine, discuss philosophy and other topics, and enjoy entertainment such as singing and dancing
**temenos**: "set apart," a sacred enclosure, marked out in some way as separate from the landscape around it
**thargelos**: the panspermia stew or bread offered to Apollon at the Thargelia festival in Athens
**theoxenia**: a banquet held in a god's honor, at which the gods and humans are thought to be feasting together
**thiasos** (pl. thiasoi): a group of worshippers of one particular god, originally in reference to Dionysos but now applicable to any god/dess
**thusia**: sacrifice, usually animal sacrifice
**xenia**: hospitality, kindness to strangers and foreigners

*Phrases for ritual*

**Khaire/Khairete** [sing./pl.]: Greetings, hello (literally: rejoice)
**Elthe deuro**: Come here (using the imperative with the gods is not, as it might seem to some people, inappropriate or overly demanding, it is in fact the traditional form for prayer)
**Klue/Kluete** [sing./pl.] **mou**: Hear me
**Hiketeuo**: I supplicate
**Eukhomai**: I pray
**Eukhomai pasi tois theois**: I pray to all the gods
**Euxamenos agalma to theo anatithesi** [past tense: **anetheke**]: I dedicate [dedicated] this as a votive offering to the god (or replace "to theo" with "**tois theois**" for more than one god).
**Ei boulei**: Please (literally, "if you wish")
**Kharin ekho**: Thank you (literally, "I have gratitude")

Examples of simple prayer:
**O Zeu, dos moi hugieian**: Zeus, give me good health.
**Nun d'aute soter isthi kai paionios, anax Apollon**: Now be my savior and my healer, lord Apollon.

## Gods' names

Below are the ancient Greek, then the English transliterations of the nominative cases (where the god is the subject of a sentence) followed by the vocative cases (where the god is being addressed directly) for some of the major deities (with accented syllables marked).

[Ζευς] Zéus : Zéu
[Ηρα] Héra : Héra
[Αθηνη] Athéne : Athéne
[Απολλων] Apóllon : Ápollon
[Αρτεμις] Ártemis : Ártemis
[Ποσειδων] Poseidón : Póseidon
[Αφροδιτη] Aphrodíte : Aphrodíte
[Ερμης] Hermés : Hermé
[Ηφαιστος] Héphaistos : Héphaiste
[Αρης] Áres : Áres
[Δημητηρ] Deméter : Deméter
[Διονυσος] Diónusos : Diónuse
[Εστια] Hestía : Hestía
[Ασκληπιος] Asklepiós : Asklepié
[Αιδης] Háides : Háide
[Εκατη] Hekáte : Hekáte
[Παν] Pán : Pán
[Περσεφονη] Persephóne : Persephóne

Pronunciation notes: The e's in Hera, Athene, Aphrodite, Hephaistos, Ares, Haides and Demeter, and the last e in Hermes, Persephone and Hekate, are all etas, meaning they make a long "ay" sound. The second o's in Poseidon and Apollon are omegas (only in the nominative case), meaning they sound like the o in "grow."

# APPENDIX IV.
## Results from the Hellenic Polytheist Survey

This survey was conducted online during the month of December, 2007, publicized on various Hellenic polytheist e-lists, forums, and by word of mouth. It was open to anyone who considers him/herself a Hellenic polytheist or who primarily worships gods from the Greek pantheon. Thus, it is a snapshot of a self-defined community, rather than one defined by myself or anyone else.

This survey was launched as an update of the 2004 survey from the first edition of this book, though some questions were changed or added. Although it has only been a few years, it appears that the Hellenic polytheist community is still in a period of growth and change. Where relevant, I have included notes on significant changes from the 2004 survey.

Not everyone answered every question, so percentages are based on the number of respondents for each question. For the open-ended questions, I tried to group the responses into general statements, and follow those with the number of people whose responses fit. Some of the unique responses follow, with no number next to them. Not all responses are verbatim, some I have summarized. For the open-ended questions, I did not print every response, but a varied selection.

**Total Respondents: 166**

**Age:**
under 18: 1%
18-24: 20%
25-29: 17%
30-39: 30%
40-49: 19%
50-59: 10%
60 or over: 4%

**Gender:**
female: 54%
male: 43%
transgendered: 2%

**Race** *(multiple selections allowed)*:
Caucasian/White: 92%
African-American/Black: 4%
Native American: 3%
Hispanic/Latino: 2%
Asian: 1%
Other: 4%

**Sexual Orientation:**
heterosexual: 55%
homosexual: 18%
bisexual: 23%
other: 4%

**Marital Status:**
single: 35%
married (legally): 37%
married (spiritually but not legally): 5%
live with partner: 5%
long term relationship: 10%
polyamorous relationship: 5%
other: 3%
*[There was a significant increase since 2004 in those married legally, and a decrease in those living with a partner.]*

**Religion of partner(s), if applicable** *(multiple selections allowed)*:
Christianity: 21%
Judaism: 5%
Islam: 0%
Buddhism: 3%
Hellenic Polytheism: 25%
Other Paganism: 22%
No Religion: 18%
Atheist: 8%
Other: 20% (included several answering Unitarian Universalist, Deist, and Agnostic, among others)

**Do you have children?**
Yes: 29%
No: 71%

**If you have children, are you raising them in your religion?**
Yes: 52%
No: 48%
*[This even split is a significant change from 2004, when over two-thirds of people answered yes.]*

**What state do you live in?** *(numbers in parentheses represent actual respondents, not percentages)*
Arizona (1); Arkansas (2); California (10); Colorado (1); Connecticut (2); Delaware (1); Florida (8); Georgia (3); Illinois (4); Indiana (5); Kansas (1); Kentucky (3); Louisiana (5); Maryland (7); Massachusetts (9); Michigan (6); Minnesota (5); Missouri (2); Nevada (2); New Hampshire (2); New Jersey (3); New Mexico (2); New York (3); North Carolina (3); Ohio (5); Oklahoma (2); Oregon (5); Pennsylvania (8); Rhode Island (2); South Dakota (2); Tennessee (3); Texas (9); Utah (1); Virginia (5); Washington (2); Wisconsin (2)

**If you live outside the United States, which country?**
Canada (9); United Kingdom (7); Australia (4); Spain (2); France (1); Ireland (1); New Zealand (1); Belgium (1); Greece (1); Turkey (1); Germany (1); Netherlands (1)

**What type of area do you live in?**
rural: 8%
small/medium town: 25%
medium/large city: 29%
suburb: 16%
large metropolitan area: 22%

**What is the highest level of education you have completed?**
some high school: 2%
high school diploma/GED: 7%
some college: 33%
bachelor's degree: 33%
master's degree: 10%
professional/technical degree: 7%
some postgraduate work: 5%
doctorate: 5%

**If you have a college degree, was it in a field related to Hellenic paganism?**
Yes: 9%
No: 72%
Somewhat: 20%

**What is your occupation?** *(Write-in)*
student (20)
computers (17)
retail / food service (12)
artist/craftsperson/writer/musician (10)
professor/teacher (9)
administrative, misc. professional (9)
health/wellbeing (6)
manager (6)
minister/counselor (5)
homemaker (5)
office worker / receptionist (4)
sciences (4)
civil servant (4)
customer service (3)
sales / marketing (3)
human resources (3)
retired (3)
editor (3)
unemployed (2)
accountant (2)
librarian (2)
social services (2)
consultant (2)
other responses included:
grantwriter, nanny, tarot reader, chef, political campaign intern, disabled veteran, pension analyst, machinist, graphic designer, landscape architect, international trade analyst, police officer, attorney

**What is your annual household income?**
less than $10,000: 9%
$10,001-$20,000: 17%
$20,001-$40,000: 22%
$40,001-$60,000: 21%
$60,001-$100,000: 22%

$100,001-$200,000: 9%
more than $200,000: 1%
*[It appears that respondents have slightly higher incomes than in 2004.]*

**What political party do you affiliate yourself with?**
Democrat: 32%
Republican: 9%
Green: 11%
Libertarian: 6%
Independent: 25%
Other: 18% (mostly non-U.S. parties, several Socialists)

**Are you active in politics/social reform?**
Yes: 44%
No: 56%

**What religion were you raised in?** *(multiple selections allowed)*
Christianity: 76%
Judaism: 2%
Islam: 0%
Buddhism: 3%
Hellenic Polytheism: 1%
Other Paganism: 1%
No religion: 19%
Atheism: 5%
Other: 8%

**How many years have you been a pagan (any type)?**
under 1: 1%
1-2: 8%
3-5: 13%
5-10: 28%
10-20: 30%
more than 20: 19%

**How many years have you been a Greek-focused pagan?**
under 1: 12%
1-2: 21%
3-5: 29%
5-10: 19%
10-20: 12%
more than 20: 7%
*[These numbers reflect more respondents who have been Hellenic longer.]*

**How did you originally come to Hellenic polytheism?** *(multiple selections allowed)*
grew from a love of Greek mythology: 57%
grew from an interest in ancient history/archaeology/Classics: 40%
had a direct experience of a deity or deities: 49%
was Wiccan or neo-pagan and gradually became focused on the Greek pantheon: 37%
was practicing another Recon-type tradition but got called by the Greek gods: 4%
followed a love of one Greek god to the rest of the pantheon: 37%
other: 14% (including philosophy, ceremonial magic, having a Greek ethnic heritage)

**What do you prefer to call yourself?**
Hellenic/Greek polytheist: 27%
Hellenic/Greek pagan: 14%
Hellenic/Greek Reconstructionist: 7%
Pagan: 15%
Neo-pagan: 4%
Hellene: 1%
Hellenist: 7%
Hellenista: 0%
Dodecatheist: 2%
Hellenic/Greek Wiccan: 1%
Hellenic/Greek Witch: 2%
Wiccan: 1%
Witch: 5%
Other: 13% (including Helleniste, Greco-Egyptian syncretist, Ekklesia Antinoou, Thessalian Hellenist, Kemetic Wiccan Buddhist, Hellenic Pantheist, Olympian, Neo-Hellen, Hellenistos, Thessalian Strix Witch, Hellenic Alexandrian Witch, hard polytheistic pagan, Greco-Roman Reconstructionist, UU Hellenist, Heathen)
*[Hellenic polytheist has greatly increased in popularity, becoming the number one choice; fewer people are referring to themselves as Reconstructionists.]*

**If you consider yourself fully dual-trad or multi-trad (participating in more than one religious path simultaneously, rather than just including a god or two from another pantheon in your practice), what is the other religious path?** *(multiple selections allowed)*
Religio Romana: 11%
Kemeticism (Egyptian): 15%

Celtic Recon: 11%
Asatru/Heathenism: 16%
Slavic/Baltic polytheism: 1%
Wicca: 23%
Christianity: 4%
Judaism: 0%
Unitarian Universalist: 7%
Buddhism: 8%
Hinduism: 3%
Other: 31% (including ADF/Druidry (6), Religious Society of Friends; Santeria, Taoism (2), Animism, Sumerian Recon, Sufism, Vedism, Reclaiming Witchcraft)

**Do you consider yourself a Reconstructionist (i.e., is it your primary spiritual methodology)?**
yes: 12%
no: 23%
my practice relies on both reconstructionism and modern innovation: 65%
*[I did not give the last choice in the first survey. However, the number choosing "yes" dropped drastically from 64% to 12%, indicating a dwindling focus on Reconstructionism.]*

**Which theological stance best describes your beliefs? (Of course you can believe more than one of these tenets, but which is the most important to your spiritual worldview?)**
Hard polytheism (all gods are distinct entities): 40%
Soft polytheism (some gods may be faces of the same gods, e.g. syncreticism): 31%
Monism (all gods are emanations of one spiritual force): 8%
Duotheism (all gods are faces of one Goddess and one God): 1%
Pantheism (everything in the world has its own god or spirit): 10%
Other: 10% (including panentheism, emanationism, animism)
*[Significantly fewer hard polytheists than in 2004.]*

**How do you mainly practice?** *(multiple selections allowed)*
alone: 89%
with partner: 16%
with small group: 28%
with large group (more than 10): 14%
with various groups: 8%
*[More people are practicing with their partner or a small group.]*

**If you often practice with a group, are the other members mainly:**
Hellenic polytheists: 37%
other Recon-type polytheists: 16%
Wiccans: 33%
neo-pagans: 34%
ceremonial magicians: 4%
Unitarians: 7%
other: 22% (including Spira, Strix, Druids, agnostic, Vodou, Chaos magicians)

**Where do you mainly practice?** *(multiple selections allowed)*
home (including home altars or temple space): 93%
public indoor space: 10%
temple (not in your own home): 2%
other people's house(s): 17%
outdoors (your own property): 30%
outdoors (public parks, forests, etc.): 34%
other, please specify: 6%
*[Home is still the primary place people worship, but more people are using public spaces as well.]*

**How often do you do small devotional practices (lighting a candle or incense, a brief prayer, a libation)?**
every day: 36%
2-5 times a week: 24%
weekly: 15%
several times a month: 13%
monthly: 4%
special occasions only: 7%
never: 1%
*[There are somewhat more people doing frequent practices.]*

**How often do you do longer rituals (at least one hour) or festival days?**
every day: 0%
2-5 times a week: 4%
weekly: 5%
several times a month: 9%
monthly: 23%
special occasions only: 46%
never: 12%

**Do you ever do rituals with other Hellenic polytheists?**
frequently: 8%
sometimes: 13%
rarely: 18%
never: 62%
comments: don't know any/aren't any in my area; no one has been interested despite my efforts; belong to a local demos/eranos; at Pantheacon; with online group; at local temple; with Spira; prefer solitary practice; with partner

**Do you ever do rituals with other non-Hellenic culture-specific polytheists (Asatru, CR, Kemetic, etc.)?**
frequently: 6%
sometimes: 14%
rarely: 17%
never: 63%
comments: Celtic; Norse; Druid; don't know any; at large conventions and festivals; partner is another Recon faith; feel like a stranger with them

**Do you ever do rituals with other general pagans or Wiccans?**
frequently: 21%
sometimes: 24%
rarely: 20%
never: 35%
comments: not interested; Druid grove; am Wiccan initiate/in coven; at festivals; they are the only group I work with regularly; too different from my own practice; at Pagan Pride Day; not comfortable with them; they are my friends; active in pagan community; enjoy any well-done ritual; beliefs and practices are too different; go with what you've got; will attend but not participate; with Unitarians; celebrate the major holidays

**Do you have a patron deity?**
yes, one: 30%
yes, more than one: 53%
no: 16%

**Do you mainly do rituals/devotions for all the gods or just a few?**
all: 15%
few: 48%
both: 37%

**Do you do rituals/devotions for any of the following?** *(% of respondents marking yes)*
nymphs: 35%
pan-Hellenic heroes (Herakles, Theseus, etc.): 29%
local heroes from your area or country: 22%
ancestors: 61%
agathos daimon: 30%
the dead (non-relations): 45%
Hestia: 71%
Titans: 14%
the Muses: 36%
*[Hestia and ancestors are still the most popular selections.]*

**Do you have an altar or shrine?**
yes, one: 34%
yes, several: 53%
no: 13%
*[More people with several shrines rather than just one.]*

**Do you follow the ancient Athenian festival calendar?**
yes, entirely: 2%
some of the festivals: 55%
no: 43%
*[Hardly anyone following it entirely, down from a quarter of respondents in 2004, which suggests more people are innovating and creating new festivals.]*

**Do you celebrate any non-Athenian ancient Greek festivals from other areas?**
yes: 41%
no: 59%

**Have you created any new festivals?**
yes: 22%
no: 54%
in the process: 19%
my group did: 5%

**Do you have a religious name (not just a screen name, but one that you use in real-world worship)?**
yes, a Greek name: 22%
yes, a non-Greek name: 19%

no, haven't found the right one yet: 19%
no, don't intend to take one: 40%

**Do you dress in ancient style clothing for rituals?**
always: 2%
sometimes: 22%
major festivals only: 6%
only when leading public rituals: 7%
never: 63%

**Do you know the ancient Greek language?**
know a little: 29%
familiar: 10%
fluent: 4%
no, not interested: 25%
no, but want to learn: 33%

**Do you use ancient Greek in ritual?**
always: 2%
sometimes: 11%
a few ritual phrases: 30%
no, but I would if I knew it: 28%
no, I prefer to only use my native language: 30%

**Do you usually observe customs concerned with miasma and ritual purity?**
yes, as if every ritual was in a temple: 7%
yes, I use khernips before every major ritual: 24%
sometimes, depending on the nature of the ritual: 28%
only when purity is a significant aspect of the ritual: 21%
no, it isn't practical in my life: 14%
no, I don't believe those rules are relevant anymore: 6%

**Do you practice any forms of divination?**
yes: 82%
no: 18%

**If so, what types do you use?** *(multiple selections allowed)*
*[options re-ordered to show most popular answers first]*
Tarot: 77%
dreams: 56%
oracular trance/direct inspiration: 35%

runes: 34%
astrology: 28%
pendulum: 28%
scrying: 21%
Limyran oracle: 20%
cleromancy (dice/lots/etc.): 18%
divinatory cards (other than Tarot): 18%
bibliomancy: 16%
Homeric oracle: 15%
augury (bird flights): 14%
tea leaves/coffee grounds: 12%
I Ching: 11%
system I invented myself: 7%
dowsing: 5%
gematria: 5%
palmistry: 5%
other: 9% (including obi, ogham, astragali, numerology, Tibetan divination, druid sticks)

**Do you practice any other kinds of 'magic' (however you define that word)?** *(multiple selections allowed)*
yes, ancient Greek methods: 16%
yes, other systems: 54%
no, not interested: 28%
no, don't know how: 14%

**How do you feel about mysticism?**
I practice it: 60%
fine for others but not interested personally: 37%
don't feel comfortable with it: 2%
strongly disagree with its inclusion in Hellenismos: 1%
*[A few more people practicing it, and a few less against it.]*

**Do you think Hellenismos should have priests?**
yes: 35%
no: 4%
not sure: 26%
only if we have temples: 20%
exegetai (advisors) are enough: 15%
*[Fewer people think we should have priests than did in 2004.]*

**What are your thoughts on reviving the practice of animal sacrifice, assuming it's done humanely as possible and most of the animal is eaten, as it was done in ancient times?**
totally support it: 28%
fine as long as you live on a farm or the animals were already going to be slaughtered: 27%
not sure: 13%
somewhat uncomfortable with the idea: 14%
totally against it: 9%
against killing animals in any context: 8%

**Have you ever made a pilgrimage to Greece to visit the sacred sites?**
yes, once: 11%
yes, more than once: 5%
no, but hope to someday: 81%
no, not interested: 3%

**Are you on any Hellenic polytheist online mailing lists or forums?**
yes: 90%
no: 10%

**Do you belong to any online-only thiasoi, demoi, eranoi, etc.?**
yes: 39%
no: 61%

**Do you have your own website (or blog) dedicated *primarily* to Hellenic polytheism?**
yes: 20%
no: 76%
my group does: 8%

**What are your favorite primary sources on Hellenic religion? (Primary sources are those written in ancient times, such as Plutarch, Euripides and Plato.)**
*[re-ordered to show popularity of answers, showing number of responses rather than percentages]*
Homer (Iliad, Odyssey): 71
Hesiod: 43
Plato: 32
Homeric Hymns: 21
Euripides: 19

Plutarch: 17
Orphic Hymns: 16
Pausanias: 14
Aeschylus: 10
Sophocles: 7
Sallustius: 6
Aristotle: 6
Herodotus: 6
Apollodoros: 5
Iamblichus: 5
Julian: 4
Callimachus: 3
Ovid: 3
Sappho: 3
Proclus: 3
Plotinus: 2
Aristophanes: 2
Cicero: 2
Pindar: 2
Celsus: 2
Apuleius: 2
Greek magical papyri: 2
Single mentions include: Xenophon; Athenaeus; Parmenides; Pythagoras; Herakleitos; Aesop; Porphyry; Marcus Aurelius; inscriptions

**What are your favorite secondary sources on Hellenic religion? (Secondary sources are written by scholars studying ancient religion, such as Burkert, Nilsson, etc. Also includes authors writing about the modern practice of Hellenismos.)**
*[re-ordered to show popularity of answers, showing number of responses rather than percentages]*
Walter Burkert: 68
Karl Kerenyi: 33
Sarah Kate Istra Winter (Oinokhoe): 20
Walter Otto: 14
Martin Nilsson: 12
H. Jeremiah Lewis (Sannion): 11
Drew Campbell: 8
Jennifer Larson: 6
Jon D. Mikalson: 5
Sarah Iles Johnston: 5

Timothy J. Alexander: 5
Jane Ellen Harrison: 4
Robert Parker: 3
Ginette Paris: 3
Mary Lefkowitz: 3
Thomas Bulfinch: 3
Peter Kingsley: 3
Lewis Richard Farnell: 2
Sue Blundell: 2
Ken Dowden: 2
Roberto Calasso: 2
Robert Graves: 2
Ross Shepherd Kraemer: 2
Marvin Meyer: 2
Robert Von Rudloff: 2
Susan Cole: 2
Jean Pierre Vernant: 2
Robin Lane Fox: 2
Single mentions include: Hearthstone; Kallistos; Philippe Borgeaud; Giulia Sissa; M. L. West; P. M. Fraser; Royston Lambert; Christine Downing; Charles Stein; Pierre Hadot; Ramsay MacMullen; Barry Strauss; Victor Hanson; Robert Turcan; Erika Simon; Robert Flaceliere; H.W. Parke; Christopher Faraone; Joan Breton Connelly; Fritz Graf; Robert Garland; Thomas Taylor; Stephanie Budin
*[Burkert and Kerenyi are still on top, Campbell has moved down the list to make way for more current authors.]*

## What are your favorite Hellenic polytheist websites?
*[re-ordered to show popularity of answers, showing number of responses rather than percentages]*
Theoi.com: 31
Sannion's Sanctuary: 29
Neokoroi: 20
Sponde: 17
Wildivine: 14
Hellenion: 14
Neos Alexandria: 12
Ta Hiera/ECauldron: 12
Kyklos Apollon: 7
Temenos Theon: 5
Winterscapes: 4
Temenos Olympicos/Shadow of Olympus: 3

Thiasos Lusios: 2
Cataleos: 2
Shrine of the Goddess Athena: 2
TempleApollo: 2
Biblioteca Arcana: 2
Sacred-Texts: 2
HTAZP: 2
Single mentions include: Julian Society; Prometheus Trust; Dadoukhoi; Elaion; HMEPA; Hekate.nu; Omphalos; Hercules Invictus; Antinopolis; SpiraCanada.com; HellenicRecons yahoogroup; HellenicPagan yahoogroup; Encyclopedia Mythica; Perseus Project; Eocto; Mind-n-Magick; WarGoddess; Hyperborean Proto-Demos; AOTSC.TDC Hellenic Fellowships

**What do you think is the most important challenge facing our religion today?**
- building real-life community: 19
- others taking us seriously: 14
- visibility: 9
- building temples or public places to worship: 8
- factions, arguing, infighting: 8
- monotheistic religions: 8
- that we live so far apart from each other: 7
- we need higher numbers: 7
- adapting ancient practices to a modern setting: 6
- clergy/priests: 4
- personality issues, egos, elitism: 4
- New Agers/neo-paganism/eclecticism: 4
- help for newcomers: 3
- integrating religion into our daily lives: 3
- "overcoming two millennia of misinformation"
- "developing long-lasting rites and rituals for the next generation"
- "to overcome dogmatic or condescending attitudes towards those who aren't practicing the 'right way'; to be more accepting of differences within our own tradition, as well as other pagan paths"
- "getting more of us into a truly deep spiritual practice"
- "information that has become lost over the millennia"
- "Reconstructionist religions need to grow to appeal to people who aren't scholars"

- "throwing off the image that we are a group of old academics who dress up at the weekends, and show people that we are a vibrant, modern and relevant religion"

## What are your hopes for the future of Hellenismos?
- temples: 26
- to be widely known/accepted: 21
- strong community: 10
- large festivals/group rituals: 10
- continued growth: 14
- people becoming united: 6
- more books, resources: 5
- clergy/priests/advisors: 4
- that it will become legal in Greece: 4
- rebuild temples and/or worship at holy sites: 4
- more people close together: 3
- to have guidance for beginners: 2
- "that we create something strong enough to be passed down to future generations, and that people come to know the gods"
- "that Hellenismos will take its place as a fully respected religion and begin to again assume its role as the major influence on the culture and wisdom of the world"
- "with the Gods with us, who can be against us?"
- "legal rites of passage carried out by the priest/priestesses of the religion"
- "that it remain true to what it is and avoids the new age and fluff"
- "Swarms of joyous celebrants marching through the city streets to honor the gods on their special day of festival... that's what I want to see."
- "develop a relationship with other recon and non-recon pagan traditions"
- "I hope to see the rise of the syncretic Hellenismos expanding and forming the many branches of Hellenismos"
- "that it grows and relaxes a little in the process, becoming a little more open and tolerant of modern approaches to old practices or of mysticism"
- "a large, mainstream religion. 'Merry Panathenaia' cards at gift shops"

- "an emphasis on 'feeling' your religion. I made the mistake of getting very into the scholarly works in the beginning, and my time was spent studying, but not feeling a connection with my deities. When I began my ritual of twice daily libations and prayers, I got so much more from that than from any book!"
- "that we can come to a place where we are informed by the successes of our ancestors but free to re-discover that which is relevant and meaningful to our modern culture"

**Any additional comments:**
- "I wish there were more concise and useful websites online that are set up clearly and explain how to perform different rituals and celebrate different festivals. I feel often as if I am stumbling through it."
- "I want the Elgin Marbles repatriated to the Acropolis museum! Praise Athene!"
- "The animal sacrifice issue is interesting. In general, under the conditions proposed, I would fully support it. What makes me hesitate is the perception people both within and outside of Hellenic Paganism would have of this practice."
- "Although I am not opposed to priests in Hellenismos, I personally do not need a priesthood to give my practice validation. In general, I'm suspicious of religions that are organized to look more like corporations than frameworks of spiritual practice."
- "I think people have a big problem with the amount of internet email lists the community has… I really do think they serve a very important purpose. No one exists in a vacuum, and when people are as scattered as we are as a group, it's vitally important to have a support center there to learn and grow from, especially when you're first starting down this path."

# BIBLIOGRAPHY

\* *recommended as foundational reading*
†*Hellenic polytheist author*

Adkins, Lesley, and Roy A. Adkins. *Handbook to Life in Ancient Greece*. Oxford: Oxford University Press, 1997.
Albinus, Lars. *The House of Hades: Studies in Ancient Greek Eschatology*. Denmark: Aarhus University Press, 2000.
Anderson, Warren D. *Music and Musicians in Ancient Greece*. Ithaca, NY: Cornell University Press, 1997.
†Bibliotheca Alexandrina, eds. *Written in Wine: A Devotional Anthology for Dionysos*. Bibliotheca Alexandrina, 2008.
Broad, William J. *The Oracle: The Lost Secrets and Hidden Message of Ancient Delphi*. New York: Penguin Press, 2006.
\*Burkert, Walter. *Greek Religion*. Translated by John Raffan. Cambridge: Harvard University Press, 1985.
_____. *Homo Necans: The Anthropology of Ancient Greek Sacrificial Ritual and Myth*. Translated by Peter Bing. Berkeley: University of California Press, 1983.
_____. *Ancient Mystery Cults*. Cambridge, MA: Harvard University Press, 1987.
Buxton, Richard, ed. *Oxford Readings in Greek Religion*. Oxford: Oxford University Press, 2001.
Calasso, Roberto. *The Marriage of Cadmus and Harmony*. New York: Vintage, 1993.
†Campbell, Drew. *Old Stones, New Temples*. Xlibris, 2000.
\*Connelly, Joan Breton. *Portrait of a Priestess: Women and Ritual in Ancient Greece*. Princeton, NJ: Princeton University Press, 2007.
Cosmopoulos, Michael B., ed. *Greek Mysteries: The Archaeology and Ritual of Ancient Greek Secret Cults*. London: Routledge, 2003.
Curnow, Trevor. *The Oracles of the Ancient World: A Comprehensive Guide*. Duckworth Publishers, 2004.
†Dawe, Jolene. *Treasures from the Deep*. Lulu.com, 2005.
Detienne, Marcel and Guilia Sissa. *The Daily Life of the Greek Gods*. Translated by Janet Lloyd. Stanford, Calif: Stanford University Press, 2000.
†Diotima. *The Goat Foot God*. Bibliotheca Alexandrina, 2008.

*Dodds, E.R. *The Greeks and the Irrational*. Berkeley: University of California Press, 1951.

Driver, Tom. *Liberating Rites: Understanding the Transformative Power of Ritual*. Boulder: Westview Press, 1998.

Erskine, Helen, ed. *To the Gods of Hellas: Lyrics of the Greek Games at Barnard College*. New York: Columbia University Press, 1930.

Evelyn-White, Hugh G., trans. *Hesiod, Homeric Hymns, Epic Cycle and Homerica*. Cambridge: Harvard University Press, 1936.

Faraone, Christopher, ed. *Initiation in Ancient Greek Rituals and Narratives*. New York: Routledge, 2003.

*Farnell, Lewis Richard. *Cults of the Greek States*. Oxford: Clarendon Press, 1896.

Festugiere, Andre-Jean. *Personal Religion Among the Greeks*. University of California Press: 1960.

Flaceliere, Robert. *Greek Oracles*. Translated by Douglas Garman. New York: W.W. Norton & Co., 1965.

*Flower, Michael. *The Seer in Ancient Greece*. University of California Press, 2008.

†Frye, Samantha. *The Golden Lyre* and *The Flaming Phoenix*, Lulu.com, 2007.

Furley, William D. and Jan Maarten Bremer. *Greek Hymns: Selected Cult Songs from the Archaic to the Hellenistic period*. Tubingen: Mohr Siebeck, 2001

*Garland, Robert. *The Greek Way of Death*. Ithaca, NY: Cornell University Press, 2001.

*_____. *The Greek Way of Life*. Ithaca, NY: Cornell University Press, 1992.

Graf, Fritz. *Magic in the Ancient World*. Cambridge, MA: Harvard University Press, 1999.

Grimal, Pierre. *The Dictionary of Classical Mythology*. Translated by A.R. Maxwell-Hyslop. New York: Basil Blackwell Publisher, 1986.

Guthrie, W.K.C. *Orpheus and Greek Religion*. New York: Norton, 1966.

*_____. *The Greeks and Their Gods*. Boston: Beacon Press, 1950.

Hagg, Robin, ed. *Ancient Greek Cult Practice From the Epigraphical Evidence*. Stockholm : Svenska Institutet i Athen, 1994.

_____. *Ancient Greek Hero Cult*. Stockholm : Svenska Institutet i Athen, 1999.

Halliday, W.R. *Greek Divination: a study of its methods and principles*. Chicago: Argonaut, 1967.

Harrison, Jane. *Prolegomena to the Study of Greek Religion*. New York: Meridian Books, 1960.

_____. *Themis: A Study of the Social Origins of Greek Religion.* Cleveland: Meridian Books, 1962.

†Hearthstone. *Devotion: Prayers to the Gods of the Greeks.* Lulu.com, 2005.

Homer. *The Iliad* and *The Odyssey.* Translated by Robert Fagles. New York: Viking, 1996.

Johnston, Sara Iles. *The Restless Dead.* Berkeley: University of California Press, 1999.

*Kerenyi, Karl. *Gods of the Greeks.* London: Thames and Hudson, 1998.

_____. *Dionysus: Archetypal Image of Indestructible Life.* Translated by Ralph Manheim. Princeton, NJ: Princeton University Press, 1976.

_____. *Eleusis: Archetypal Image of Mother and Daughter.* Translated by Ralph Manheim. Princeton, NJ: Princeton University Press, 1967.

_____. *Hermes: Guide of Souls.* Translated by Murray Stein. Woodstock, CT: Spring Publications, 1976.

Kingsley, Peter. *In the Dark Places of Wisdom.* The Golden Sufi Center, 1999.

Kurtz, Donna and John Boardman. *Greek Burial Customs.* London: Thames and Hudson, 1971.

*Larson, Jennifer. *Greek Nymphs.* Oxford: Oxford University Press, 2001.

* _____. *Ancient Greek Cults: A Guide.* New York: Routledge, 2007.

_____. *Greek Heroine Cults.* University of Wisconsin Press, 1995.

Lawson, John Cuthbert. *Modern Greek Folklore and Ancient Greek Religion.* Cambridge: University Press, 1910

†*Lewis, H. Jeremiah. *A Temple of Words: Essays Culled from Five Years of Sannion's Sanctuary.* Cafepress, 2005.

† _____. *Gods and Mortals: New Stories of Hellenic Polytheism.* Bibliotheca Alexandrina, 2008.

Luck, Georg. *Arcana Mundi: Magic and the Occult in the Greek and Roman Worlds.* Baltimore: Johns Hopkins University Press, 1985.

Meyer, Marvin W., ed. *The Ancient Mysteries: A Sourcebook.* San Francisco: HarperSanFrancisco, 1987.

Mikalson, Jon D. *Honor Thy Gods: Popular Religion in Greek Tragedy.* Chapel Hill, NC: University of North Carolina Press, 1991.

†Minai, Thista. *Dancing in Moonlight: Understanding Artemis through Celebration.* Asphodel Press, 2008.

†Neokoroi, eds. *He Epistole: A Collection of Issues #1-12.* Cafepress, 2007.

*Nilsson, Martin. *Greek Folk Religion*. Philadelphia: University of Pennsylvania Press, 1961.

———. *A History of Greek Religion*. Translated by F.J. Fielden. New York: W.W. Norton & Co., 1964.

———. *Greek Piety*. Translated by Herbert Rose. New York: W.W. Norton & Co., 1969.

Ogden, Daniel. *Greek and Roman Necromancy*. Princeton, NJ: Princeton University Press, 2001.

*The Orphic Hymns*. Translated by Apostolos N. Athanassakis. Atlanta: Scholars Press, 1988.

Otto, Walter F. *Dionysus: Myth and Cult*. Translated by Robert B. Palmer. Dallas: Spring Publications, 1989.

*———. *The Homeric Gods*. Boston: Beacon Press, 1954.

Palmer, Leonard R. *Mycenaeans and Minoans*. New York: Alfred A. Knopf, 1965.

*Parke. H.W. *Festivals of the Athenians*. London: Thames and Hudson, 1977.

Parker, Robert. *Miasma: Pollution and Purification in Early Greek Religion*. Oxford: Oxford University Press, 1990.

———. *Polytheism and Society at Athens*. Oxford: Oxford University Press, 2005.

*Pausanias. *Guide to Greece*. Translated by Peter Levi. New York: Penguin Books, 1979.

Pollard, John. *Seers, Shrines and Sirens*. New York: A.S. Barnes and Co., 1965.

Price, Simon. *Religions of the Ancient Greeks*. Cambridge: Cambridge University Press, 1999.

*Pulleyn, Simon. *Prayer in Greek Religion*. New York: Oxford University Press, 1997.

Rohde, Erwin. *Psyche: The Cult of Souls and Belief in Immortality Among the Greeks*. New York: Harcourt & Brace, 1925.

Rouse, William H.D. *Greek Votive Offerings*. Cambridge: Cambridge University Press, 1902.

Scully, Vincent. *The Earth, the Temple and the Gods: Greek Sacred Architecture*. New Haven: Yale University Press, 1962.

Shorter, Bani. *Susceptible to the Sacred: The Psychological Experience of Ritual*. London: Routledge, 1996.

Simon, Erika, *Festivals of Attica*. University of Wisconsin, 1983.

Spawforth, Tony. *The Complete Greek Temples*. London: Thames & Hudson Ltd., 2006.

Steiner, Deborah Tarn. *Images in Mind: Statues in Archaic and Classical Greek Literature and Thought*. Princeton, NJ: Princeton University Press, 2002.

†Szabo, Allyson. *Longing for Wisdom: The Message of the Maxims*. Bibliotheca Alexandrina, 2008.

Van Straten, F.T. *Hiera Kala: Images of Animal Sacrifice in Archaic and Classical Greece*. Brill Academic Publishers, 1995.

Vernant, Jean-Pierre, and Pierre Vidal-Naquet. *Myth and Tragedy in Ancient Greece*. New York: Zone Books, 1990.

Versnel, H.S., ed. *Faith Hope and Worship: Aspects of Religious Mentality in the Ancient World*. Brill Academic Publishers, 1981.

*Zaidman, Louise Bruit, and Pauline Schmitt Pantel. *Religion in the Ancient Greek City*. Translated by Paul Cartledge. Cambridge: Cambridge University Press, 1999

# INTERNET RESOURCES

## Hellenic Polytheism Websites

- **Kharis** - *winterscapes.com/kharis/* - the website for this book, includes links to many other resources. Also check out my homepage, *winterscapes.com*, for a list of all my websites.
- **Sannion's Sanctuary** - *winterscapes.com/sannion/* - includes essays, poetry, hymns, retelling of myths, etc.
- **Neokoroi** - *neokoroi.org* - organization for Hellenic polytheists, they publish the quarterly newsletter *He Epistole* (back issues available online for free)
- **Hands-On Hellenism (Sponde.com)** - *sponde.suneagle.info* - great resource, lots of advice
- **HMEPA** - *numachi.com/~ccount/hmepa/* - a very useful resource that aligns the ancient festival calendar with our modern one
- **Hellenion** - *hellenion.org* - a non-profit organization for Hellenic pagans, parent of a few demoi and proto-demoi, has clergy training program
- **Thiasoi Directory** - *winterscapes.com/thiasoi.htm* - listings for most Hellenic pagan organizations, regional groups, god-based mailing lists, etc.
- **Neos Alexandria** - *neosalexandria.org* - Graeco-Egyptian syncretic group, includes online temples, extensive essays, Bibliotheca Alexandrina publishing imprint
- **Kyklos Apollon** - *kyklosapollon.org* - centered around weekly Apollon purification ritual, discussion group
- **The Dionysion** - *hermeticfellowship.org/Dionysion/* - filled with the fruits of extensive research into topics like the maenads, ecstasy, theatre and more.
- **Cataleos** - *cataleos.org* - website for a physical temple space for Artemis - articles, events, etc. Also see **HTAZP** - *worship.htazp.org* - a temple site for Apollon, Zeus and Pan.
- **Greek Alphabet Oracle** - *cs.utk.edu/~Mclennan/BA/LAO.html* - formerly called the Limyran Oracle, an ancient divination system translated and interpreted. Part of the larger Biblioteca Arcana website.

## Other Websites of Interest

- Perseus Project - *perseus.tufts.edu* - online collection of ancient texts from Greece and Rome, shown bilingually, includes dictionary and other resources
- Theoi Greek Mythology - *theoi.com* - extensive reference site on Greek mythology and religion
- The Ancient Library - *ancientlibrary.com* - scanned books on topics relating to ancient history
- Women in Greek Myths - *paleothea.com* - an encyclopedia of female figures in Greek mythology
- Ancient Greek Religion - *greekreligion.org* - a vast collection of links to sites covering all aspects of ancient Hellenic polytheism
- The Oracle of Delphi and Ancient Oracles - *isidore-of-seville.com/oracles* - information on important ancient oracles
- Internet Sacred Text Archive - *sacred-texts.com* - collection of online books about religion, mythology, folklore, the esoteric
- Greece Travel - *greecetravel.com* - a guide to visiting Greece

## Ritual Supplies

- Art from Greece (statues, pottery, reliefs, etc.) - *artfromgreece.com*
- Hellenic Art (same as above) - *hellenic-art.com*
- Sacred Source (replica statues) - *sacredsource.com*
- Magical Omaha (modern statues) - *magicalomaha.com/Greekgodgoddessstatury.htm*
- Mid-East Instruments - *mid-east.com*
- Projekt (music label, home to Daemonia Nymphe) - *projekt.com*

## Language Reference and Used/Out-of-Print Books

- Ancient Greek Tutorials - *socrates.berkeley.edu/~ancgreek/*
- Anamathetes: Hellenic polytheists learning ancient Greek - *groups.yahoo.com/group/anamathetes/*
- Schoenhof's Foreign Books - *schoenhofs.com*
- Advanced Book Exchange (used books) - *abebooks.com*
- Kessinger Publishing (reprints of old books) - *kessinger.net*

# ABOUT THE AUTHOR

Sarah Kate Istra Winter, also known by her religious name Oinokhoe, has been practicing Hellenic polytheism for over ten years; she is devoted to Dionysos, Hermes, Apollon and the Nymphs. Ms. Winter has written for a number of pagan publications, and was the editor of the Neokoroi newsletter *He Epistole* for several years. She holds a Bachelor's degree in Myth and Ritual from Goddard College.

Ms. Winter is the founder of Thiasos Lusios (an online Dionysian group), co-founder of the Eranos Agriotheios (Wildivine), and the owner of several polytheist websites which can be found at her homepage, winterscapes.com. She grew up in New England, and now lives in beautiful Eugene, Oregon, where nymphs can be found around every corner.

Printed in Germany
by Amazon Distribution
GmbH, Leipzig